20 YEARS OF SOUTH AFRICAN DEMOCRACY

SO WHERE TO NOW?

This research project was supported by:

Thabo Mbeki
FOUNDATION

THABO MBEKI AFRICAN LEADERSHIP INSTITUTE

Investing in Thought Leaders for Africa's Renewal

UNISA
university
of south africa

FRIEDRICH
EBERT
STIFTUNG
South Africa Office

20 YEARS OF SOUTH AFRICAN DEMOCRACY

SO WHERE TO NOW?

MAPUNGUBWE
INSTITUTE FOR STRATEGIC REFLECTION (MISTRA)

MAPUNGUBWE
INSTITUTE FOR STRATEGIC REFLECTION (MISTRA)

Mapungubwe Institute for Strategic Reflection (MISTRA)
First floor, Cypress Place North
Woodmead Business Park
142 Western Service Road
Woodmead 2191
Johannesburg

First published October 2015

© MISTRA 2015

ISBN 978-1-920655-23-5

Published by Real African Publishers
on behalf of the Mapungubwe Institute for Strategic Reflection
(MISTRA)

PO Box 3317
Houghton
Johannesburg 2041

REAL AFRICAN PUBLISHERS

Sub-editor: Barry Gilder
Copy editor: Angela McClelland

MAPUNGUBWE INSTITUTE (MISTRA)
[A NON-PROFIT COMPANY][104-474-NPO]
REGISTRATION NUMBER 2010/002262/08
["THE INSTITUTE"]

CONTENTS

PREFACE

This publication is the outcome of a conference – marking the beginning of South Africa's third decade of democracy – hosted in November 2014 by the Mapungubwe Institute for Strategic Reflection (MISTRA) and the Thabo Mbeki African Leadership Institute (TMALI) at the University of South Africa (Unisa). The conference was entitled *20 Years of South African Democracy: So Where to Now?*

In the twenty years since South Africa made the transition from apartheid to democracy, much had been achieved to transform society, informed by the injunctions of the Constitution, which formally guarantees equal opportunities without regard to race, gender and other social fault-lines. This period has seen some improvements in people's quality of life and tentative steps towards national unity and social cohesion. Yet, much work lies ahead in realising the aspirations of many South Africans who still experience the effects of unemployment, poverty and inequality. Much has to be done to build a capable developmental state and active citizenry able to manifest in practical terms the narrative of 'Africa Rising' on the southern tip of the continent.

The conference focused primarily on projective reflections into the next two decades of democracy, informed, firstly, by key historical moments in the build-up to the transition, and secondly, by the experiences of the last 20 years. It aimed to deal with the theoretical perspectives underpinning the state of South Africa in two decades of democracy and, most importantly, prospects for the future.

Some of the questions the conference sought to address included:

- How do we internalise with common purpose what has been learned since 1994?
- What are the remaining structural deficiencies to be overcome in order to lead to growth with development?
- What can be done to translate the vision and programmes of the National Development Plan into purposeful action by all stakeholders?
- What is the dynamic relationship between national unity, social cohesion and socio-economic advancement?
- Where is South Africa getting it right and wrong in terms of economic

growth and development?

- What can be learnt from other democratic transitions and countries that have sustained high economic growth rates and social inclusion?
- What is the combination of 'big ideas and bold actions' that South Africa will need to embrace to launch onto a new developmental trajectory?
- What kind of a society do the youth of today want?

The conference also dealt with the issue of 'The Global Economy and Africa's Positioning', but that is the topic of a separate MISTRA research project and its outcome is to be published in a separate volume. This publication covers the following main themes of the conference:

- Reflections on Historical Moments
- The South African Political Economy
- Values, Nation Formation and Social Compacting
- Innovation and Transdisciplinary Knowledge for Action
- Building a Capable Developmental State

Contained in this volume are inputs from a wide range of prominent South African and international thinkers, practitioners and activists. Some are in the form of prepared papers and others are taken from transcripts of presentations. They are presented in the hope that the thought-provoking and incisive discourse that took place at the conference can contribute to the continuation of a discussion that, by its nature, can have no end. The infusion of our past and our present into our future cannot help but ensure that the pertinent and pressing questions canvassed at the conference can continue to engage our minds as we grapple with the task of making our future worthy of the sacrifices of our past.

We trust that this publication will contribute to the conversation taking place about how, together, we can improve the human condition.

Joel Netshitenzhe
Executive Director: MISTRA

Vusi Gumede
Head: TMALI

ACKNOWLEDGEMENTS

The Mapungubwe Institute for Strategic Reflection (MISTRA) and the Thabo Mbeki African Leadership Institute (TMALI) express their profound gratitude to the speakers who participated in the 20 Years of South African Democracy: So Where to Now? conference and who consented to having their inputs included in this publication.

We thank the University of South Africa (Unisa) and the Thabo Mbeki Foundation for their support for the conference and the Friedrich-Ebert-Stiftung for their generous funding of the conference and this publication.

Very warm appreciation is extended to the staff of MISTRA, TMALI and Unisa who organised a logistically complex yet highly successful conference, in particular Gail Smith of MISTRA who coordinated the conference planning, preparations and implementation.

Thanks is specifically extended to Siphokazi Mdidimba of MISTRA for her assistance in sub-editing this publication, to Barry Gilder for putting the publication together and to Angela McClelland and Reedwaan Vally of Real African Publishers for copy editing, designing and producing this publication.

MISTRA extends its warm appreciation to its donors who contributed to this project as well as to those who have generally contributed to the work of the Institute.

Conference Funders
Friedrich-Ebert-Stiftung

MISTRA Donors
Corporates
Absa
Anglo American
AngloGold Ashanti
Anglo Platinum
Aspen Pharmacare
Batho Batho Trust
Chancellor House
Development Bank of South Africa
Discovery
Encha Group Limited
Kumba Iron Ore
MTN
Mvelaphanda Management Services
Power Lumens Africa
Safika
Sanral
Sasol
Shanduka Group
Simeka Group
Standard Bank
Yard Capital Development Trust
Yellowwoods

Local Foundations and Trusts
First Rand Foundation
Nedbank Foundation
Social Science Development Forum (SOSDEF)
Oppenheimer Memorial Trust

International Sources
People's Republic of China Embassy

Individuals
Thandi Ndlovu

KEYNOTE

REFLECTIONS ON SOUTH AFRICAN CONSTITUTIONAL DEMOCRACY – TRANSITION AND TRANSFORMATION – JUSTICE DIKGANG MOSENEKE

Introduction and Salutations

I salute you all, distinguished people of our great country. I am grateful to be here rather than in court this morning. I owe gratitude to the Mapungubwe Institute for Strategic Reflection (MISTRA), the Thabo Mbeki African Leadership Institute (TMALI) and special thanks to my alma mater and the only university I have ever attended and from which I acquired no less than three degrees during my short stint of ten years on Robben Island. Yes, ten years can only be a short stint if one remembers that our departed and beloved leader, Mr Nelson Rolihlahla Mandela, was there for twenty-seven years.

I have been asked to reflect on our constitutional democracy with a slant on transition and transformation. This I propose to do by looking at the past twenty years only fleetingly in order to proffer reflections on our collective future. Our hosts have urged that our dialogue in the next two days should not be diagnostic but rather prognostic. The thematic conversations at this conference seem to require of us not to analyse the past until we are hypnotised, but rather to probe the future, as Lenin famously asked: 'what's to be done?' Appropriately, we have been counselled to dwell in the past only so that we may thoughtfully pose the question: 'So where to now?'

This conference will be reflecting on selected trends and features of our democratic transition. I hope not to venture into allotted terrains of distinguished leaders, scholars and other thinkers who will be presenting in panels. Therefore, I will not recount historical moments, nor dabble in the discourse on our political economy or African economic renewal, let alone the global economy. There are others better suited to that task. Similarly, I won't debate values, nation formation and social compacting. Nor will I venture into a discussion on innovation, transdisciplinary knowledge or the prognosis for a developmental state. These matters will enjoy the attention of distinguished contributors.

I propose to stick to my knitting. I must remind myself that, although I am a child of our revolution for a just society, I am a sitting judge in the service of all our people and their democratic state. It behoves me to speak like a judge, a role I have played so long that it now feels like the only thing I have done all my life. I will describe briefly our transition and the normative scheme of our democratic enterprise. Next, in broad brush strokes, I will depict what the transition has yielded. Being a judge, I will catalogue what the courts have done in the two decades of transition. I will then turn my lens onto four selected features of our democratic project that pose trenchant challenges to the democratic project. These challenges, I think, deserve our careful reflection, as we, patriots, ask what is to be done.

The first of the challenges is the land question. Here, I will be probing whether the democratic project has secured urban and rural land justice. The second issue flows from the first. It is the vexed terrain of the achievement of equality, non-racialism and restitution. In the third instance, I will ask questions about the impact of concentrated executive power on our public institutions and, lastly, I will reflect on the mediation and adjudication of public disputes.

TRANSITION AND RESULTANT NORMATIVE SCHEME

Let me start with a touch of patriotic vanity. In the wake of the Arab Spring, a US Supreme Court Justice, Ruth Bader-Ginsberg, whilst visiting Egypt, was asked to provide advice on constitution-making. She is reported to have said: 'I would not look to the United States Constitution if I were drafting a constitution in 2012.' She recommended to the Egyptians to look, in her words, to 'the South African Constitution and perhaps the Canadian Chapter on Rights and Freedoms, and the European Convention on Human Rights'.[1]

A fascinating law journal article, 'The Declining Influence of the United States Constitution',[2] penned by two American Law Professors,[3] bemoans the decline of American constitutionalism around the world. The article reports on an empirical study of constitutions of the world and finds that four constitutions are influential benchmarks for modern constitution-making. It lists the constitutions of South Africa, Canada, Germany, and India.[4] So we can afford to be gentle on ourselves. We have managed our post-conflict arrangements better than we grant ourselves.

Our constitutional democracy was forged on the anvil of division, past injustice and economic inequity, but also on the hope for reconciliation, nation building and social cohesion. Notionally, our Constitution is premised on the will of the people expressed in representative and participatory processes. It does not only establish its supremacy, rule of law and fundamental rights but also recites our collective convictions.[5] It contains our joint and minimum ideological and normative choices of what a good society should be. It enjoins the state, and all its organs, to take reasonable steps without undue delay to achieve that good society. The virtuous society envisioned has a significant social democratic flavour, some reckon, and yet others take it to be a neo-liberal compromise. Facile tags aside, the Constitution provides for many progressive things. It protects and advances fair labour practices.[6] It compels all to preserve an environment that is not harmful for the benefit of present and future generations.[7] It envisions restitution of land to victims of dispossession but does not permit arbitrary deprivation of property. It permits expropriation and redistribution of land for public good provided that it is against just and equitable compensation.[8] The envisioned society sets itself firmly against poverty, ill health and ignorance. This it does by promising everyone the right to have access to adequate housing, healthcare, food, water and social security, subject to available resources and progressive realisation.[9] A child's best interests are of paramount importance in every matter concerning it.[10] And everyone has a right to basic education, including adult basic education.[11]

The Constitution enjoins and hopes for an effective, responsive, open and accountable governance from all organs of state, inclusive of parliament, the executive and the courts. Parliament must make laws, hold the executive accountable and provide a forum for the debate of matters of national importance. The executive must implement laws, make policy and spend fiscal allocations. Courts must resolve disputes in accordance with the Constitution and the law, which includes African indigenous law and the common law.

It must follow from what I have said that our constitutional design is emphatically transformative. It is meant to migrate us from a murky and brutish past to an inclusive future animated by values of human decency and solidarity. It contains a binding consensus on, or a blueprint for, what a fully transformed society should look like.

WHAT HAS THE TRANSITION YIELDED?

We are dismantling racial domination. We have managed a treacherous transition and set up ground rules that underscore our democratic ethos, public morality and governance. We have established and maintained a functional democratic state with all the customary markers, including multi-partyism, regular elections, and rule of law and separation of powers. Our parliamentary system functions certainly more at an elective than at a participatory level. Our fiscal and state treasury functions are not shabby and our revenue collection is world class. Our courts are independent and effective. Our Chapter 9 institutions,[12] the Auditor General, the Electoral Commission, the Human Rights Commission and the Public Protector, to name a few, have teeth and often do bite. We boast of a robust civil society that takes up social causes around just about every social issue: for instance, campaigns on HIV and Aids and access to healthcare; on genderised violence. and on access to textbooks and education. For good measure, one may add poo protests, wide-spread opposition to e-tolling, objections to the use of labour brokers and the campaign on the right to know. We have more than our fair share of open and public dissent and street protests amongst marginalised people. We are blessed with a vigilant labour movement, a free press that is prying, fearless and unbending. None of our citizens has been jailed only for political, religious or other beliefs. We are not pitted against each other in a civil war or genocide or terrorist attacks. Our transition has indeed yielded much.

If you think that is an overly rosy picture of our democratic transition, I urge you to suspend your judgement until I finish. I will shortly debate future challenges to our democracy.

WHAT VALUE HAVE THE COURTS ADDED?

In many senses our courts have been remarkable. Shortly after our transition, equality and discrimination cases proliferated. In a series of notable cases, courts have refused to tolerate inequality and discrimination.[13] They have struck down scores of laws that undermined appropriate respect for diversity or that harboured antiquated prejudices.[14] Amidst many rumblings, courts would not tolerate, for example, homophobia or gender inequality inspired by religious or cultural patriarchy. They have fashioned the notion of substantive equality that travels well beyond the liberal notion of formal equality.[15] We have insisted that laws and policy must provide for adequate protection of children, people with disability, and refugees as well as migrants, and root out domestic violence.[16]

Courts have, time without count, required the executive to give effect to the socio-economic claims of the poor and vulnerable. We have required government to provide appropriate access to health care.[17] Happily so today, our jurisdiction has arguably one of the best public treatment regimes for HIV and Aids patients. We have reminded the executive of its duty to provide access to housing.[18] We have mediated differences around the rampant eviction of homeless, urban and rural occupiers who are said to be unlawful.[19] We have insisted that landowners must display patience as homeless occupiers find other refuge.[20] Often we have ordered municipalities to engage meaningfully with communities in order to avert inhumane evictions.[21] We have ordered government to find alternative accommodation should evictions ensue.[22] Courts have insisted that drinkable water be made available to vulnerable members of society.[23] We have protected learners from being subjected to a medium of instruction they don't want.[24] We have required that learners be furnished with study material.[25] Courts have required the social grants to reach all, including vulnerable migrants, and that grants be paid promptly, particularly in the rural neighbourhoods.[26]

Our courts have developed a proud jurisprudence on justice at the work-place.[27] That is a consequence of the vital choices our founding mothers and fathers have made on worker rights, the recognition and formation of trade unions and employer organisations, the resultant collective bargaining and fair labour practices. Properly so, courts have refused to sacrifice workplace justice on the back of claims or promises of economic growth that a so-called open labour market will bring to us. That may, or may not, be so. But that is not for judges to decide. Courts are bound by labour laws. Just labour laws are integral to a more equal and caring society where the dignity of all, including of working people, is well shielded.

Courts have been properly preoccupied with the protection of the right to free expression, including a free press, and the right to impart and receive information and art.[28] Our judgments point to the intrinsic worth of free expression and the many public and private blessings of a free and open and debating society. And yet, our judgments have also warned that free expression has limits, particularly when it encroaches on dignity and privacy.[29] However, when public interest is in issue, other and perhaps more pressing considerations come to the fore. That balance is not generic: it can be properly struck only on a case-by-case basis.

Courts have intervened where valid allegations have been made about wrongful procurement of goods and services by government.[30] This is a sequel to the important requirement of our Constitution that, when all spheres of the state contract for goods and services, they must do so within a system that is fair, equitable, transparent, competitive and cost-effective.[31] To that end, Parliament is enjoined to legislate in order to prescribe an appropriate framework for a procurement policy. Of course, the Constitution was alive to the fact that government procurement practices would be vital in the achievement of a more equal society.

In the same breath, our constitutional project is properly inimical to, and intolerant of, corrupt state tender practices and all forms of public or private corruption. Courts can only deal with prosecutions that come before them and these sadly have been surprisingly few. In the last two decades, no criminal prosecutions on tender irregularities, misuse of public funds or related fraud have served before our superior courts. The celebrated cases of Selebi[32] and Shaik[33] related to private and not public funds. This begs the question: was there was no misuse of public funds or tender fraud in the last twenty years worth prosecuting? The record shows that, when the prosecuting authorities have ventured into courts, my judicial sisters and brothers have not wavered.

Competition law has found a niche in our courts. This is admirable. In the past, our economy allowed very little real competition in the market because of structural and behavioural anti-competitiveness. Some of our manufacturing and retail businesses have been found by our courts to have engaged in collusive practices, including price fixing. The Competition Commission and its tribunals have done much enviable work to remedy or reduce commercial injustices to consumers that flow from collusive pricing.[34]

TRENCHANT CHALLENGES

I turn to look at the four trenchant challenges we would do well to heed in our further democratic journey.

Land restoration, urban and rural land justice

Nearly 70 years ago, in *The Wretched of the Earth*,[35] Frantz Fanon observed that '[F]or a colonized people the most essential value, because it is the most concrete, is first and foremost the land: the land which will bring them bread and, above all, dignity'.

Fanon's remarks were apt but not a new insight, if one remembers that the organising principle at the formation of the African National Congress in 1912 was the impending wholesale land confiscation prefigured in the 1913 Land Act. The land dispossession, coupled with urban spatial apartheid, led to immeasurable social devastation recorded in many invaluable studies.[36]

The land question was foremost at the time of the formulation of the Constitution. This is displayed in the careful formulation of the property clause, which is often more maligned than carefully scrutinised.[37] Let us quickly look at the scheme of the property clause. I start with land restitution. The section envisions restitution of land to victims of dispossession but does not permit arbitrary deprivation of property. A person or community dispossessed of property after June 1913 by racially discriminatory laws is entitled to either restitution or equitable redress.[38] Similarly, a person or community whose land tenure is insecure because of apartheid laws is entitled to a secure land title.[39] Commendably, parliament passed the legislation to give effect to land restoration within twelve months of democratic rule and established a dedicated Land Claims Court.[40]

The property clause permits expropriation of land by a law of general application, provided it is for a public purpose or in the public interest, and it is against just and equitable compensation, reflecting an equitable balance between the public interest and the interest of the landowner. The extent of the compensation may be fixed by agreement or by a court guided by a number of listed factors. Let's slaughter a few shibboleths. The Constitution does not protect property. It merely protects an owner against arbitrary deprivation.[41] Deprivation that is not arbitrary is permissible. The property clause does not carry the phrase: 'willing buyer: willing seller', which is often blamed for an inadequate resolution of the land question. The state's power to expropriate does not depend on the willingness of the landowner. The compensation may be agreed but, if not, a court must fix it. The compensation must be just and equitable and not necessarily the market value of the land. Market price is but one of five criteria the Constitution lists for a court to set fair compensation.[42] The property clause is emphatic that the state must take reasonable measures, within available resources, to enable citizens to gain access to land on an equitable basis.

The cutting question is whether our democratic consolidation has achieved urban or rural land equity. Although much has been done, the answer is no. Present statistics on land redistribution show very little movement away from apartheid patterns of the use and ownership of land.[43] Only a small percentage of land restitution claims have been finalised.[44]

The bulk is yet to reach the courts.[45] Land claims that do reach the courts display remarkable delays of years before reaching the courts. The claims are also beset by bureaucratic inadequacies. And there are severe difficulties for claimants in gathering evidence to back the claims and to overcome legal resistance by some owners. On another front, there is very scant evidence of the use by government of expropriation to achieve land equity.

In twenty years, our Court has not resolved even one case of land expropriation under the property clause by government for a public purpose. Similarly, in the same time, the courts have never been called upon to give meaning to the property clause in the context of land expropriation or to decide on what is a just and equitable compensation. One would have expected that a matter so pressing as land use, occupation or ownership would pre-dominate the list of disputes in the post-conflict contestation. Sadly, urban homelessness persists. Apartheid spatial patterns remain. People in informal settlements run the risk of mass evictions such as in Lwandle in the Cape[46] or Cato Crest[47] in KwaZulu-Natal.

Rural land hunger stands in the way of genuine rural development. Women who till the soil and live on communal land don't have the protection that security of land tenure provides. Communal land vests in traditional authorities who do not always act in the best interest of their communities, made up mainly of women and children. In at least two cases relating to the platinum rich Limpopo and North-West provinces, our Court had to intervene where the traditional leaders had concluded mining arrangements on communal land without proper consultation with the traditional community.[48]

It may be that the property and restitutionary provisions in Section 25 of the Constitution on land have been hopelessly underworked. I want to suggest that we cannot talk about transformation or social justice and cohesion when urban and rural land injustice dominates the lives of a majority of our citizens. Millions will continue to live in desperately undignified conditions unless we confront land inequity.

Equality, Non-racialism and Restitution and Social Justice

The achievement of equality is a founding value of our Constitution[49] and it is said to be the most prominent organising principle of our democratic enterprise. And yet, our reality is starkly different. Several socio-economic measures suggest that we are the most unequal society on the globe. Lately, a World Bank study compared us with eleven other middle-income countries[50] and concluded that:

> *However, even with a progressive tax system, inequality in South Africa was still higher than the other eleven countries in the sample. This was because it was one of the most unequal countries in the world.*
>
> *Even though South Africa has a very effective use of its fiscal tools, the original problems in income inequality are so high that South Africa is going to need other things to help it address the problem of inequality.*
>
> *To make further progress going forward, you need to complement fiscal policy with higher more inclusive growth that essentially generates jobs, especially at the lower end of the distribution.*[51]

I must immediately add that the study commended our state for the way it has used fiscal tools to reduce poverty: 3.6 million people have been lifted above the poverty line. The use of social grants has also lowered the Gini co-efficient on income, which measures inequality.

The World Bank update talks about 'the original problem in income inequality' and that South Africa is going to need other measures to help reduce inequality. That historical inequality, of both income and wealth, still persists and, race and gender, in most instances, are markers of past exclusion or disadvantage. In order to address historical disadvantage, our equality clause permits legislative and other measures to achieve equality. These are restitutionary measures sometimes inappropriately called affirmative action. The two most prominent examples of such measures are the employment equity and black economic empowerment laws.

At the turn of two decades of our democratic project, there has been an increasing discourse about the appropriateness of restitutionary measures within a democratic project that prides itself on non-racial and non-sexist values. As I understand the one end of the argument, there is an inherent tension between the requirements of equal protection of the law and of non-racism on the one end, and affirmative action measures which are intended to benefit the previously vulnerable groups on the other. The argument is that race or gender are not always useful or accurate markers of past disadvantage. The further point is made that young people born in 1994 have no business to look to affirmative action measures because they did not live under racial disadvantage and, in any event, many middle-class black youth have been as advantaged as much as, or more than, white youth. In certain quarters, employment equity and other related matters are considered to be reverse racism.

There is indeed force in the argument that mere race or gender may not be an accurate index of social exclusion and disadvantage. We know that one of the trophies of the national democratic phase of the transition is that the African middle class has shot up from 1.8 million to 5.7 million. That may indeed appear to be an indicator of a more equal society until one locates 5.7 million within a population of 52 million people. Then the black middle class peters out to a mere 10 per cent of the population.

Of course, there is an inherent tension between transformative goals based on race and gender in the face of the constitutional value of non-racial and non-sexist equality. It is necessary that legislation and executive action is limited to permissible ameliorative measures that fall within the strict carve-out created by the Constitution itself. It clearly permits legislative and other measures to promote the achievement of equality.[52] The measures must be designed to protect or advance persons disadvantaged by unfair discrimination. The measures may not amount to quotas. They must be applied rationally and only to procure a more equal society. In the second twenty years of our democracy, we will have to think carefully about whether the measures continue to be justified. This is so because fewer and fewer people will be able to claim legitimately that they have been disadvantaged by unfair discrimination of the past. For now, the measures would enjoy constitutional protection because the Constitution permits restitutionary measures in so many words.

The time may not be far off when the national psyche may not be able to tolerate the notion that class interest may very well supersede interests forged around race, gender and past disadvantage. A last point has to be made. The most effective way of confronting past disadvantage must lie in the broader socio-economic transformative agenda. In a non-racial way we must strive for an equal and socially just society. We must harness public resources carefully towards quality education, entrepreneurial capabilities, better health care and access to housing. For instance, fiscal interventions have funded social grants for all vulnerable people irrespective of their gender or race. To conclude, our constitutional design permits ameliorative or restitutionary measures and courts are obliged to give effect to them. As I conclude I pose the question whether a race-based transformation continues to be consistent with a broader constitutional transformation. Many transformative projects in the Constitution, and in particular its socio-economic guarantees, are not race or gender based and need not be.

Executive Power and Public Institutions

Much of the glowing talk about our constitutional architecture relates to fundamental rights and freedoms. And yet, the manner in which public power is allocated within it is not always optimal for advancing our democratic project. I suggest that, in the next two decades, we may have to revisit the dispersal of public power. Because of time and space I will limit the discussion to the national executive. Of course, amending executive power may be a difficult task that calls for a constitutional amendment. Much as the Constitution is premised on principles of cooperative government[53] binding the national, provincial and local spheres of government, a careful examination of the powers of the national executive in Chapter 5 of the Constitution, and in other legislation, displays a remarkable concentration of the President's powers of appointment. In a few instances, the President exercises these powers of appointment together with Parliament and other organs of state. As for the rest, the President appoints within his exclusive discretion.

The anecdotal account is that, at the time of the formulation of the final Constitution, whenever there was a dispute about who should appoint a public functionary, the negotiating parties were happy to leave the power in the incumbent President, Nelson Mandela. He, after all, will do the right thing. In a footnote, I have rehearsed the complete catalogue of the President's powers of appointment.[54]

I refer to a few. Unlike other countries where the deputy president is a running mate, here he is appointed by the president.[55] This means he or she may be dismissed summarily by the president. Our own history has shown how the dismissal of a deputy president could be deleterious to the executive function. The president appoints the Ministers of the Cabinet and Deputy Ministers, leaders of government business to the National Assembly.[56] He appoints all ambassadors.[57] The president appoints the Chief Justice and the Deputy Chief Justice, after consultation with the Judicial Service

Commission (JSC), and appoints the President of the Supreme Court of Appeal.[58] He is also empowered to appoint the Judge President of the Land Claims Court[59] and Chairperson of the Competition Tribunal,[60] and the Judge President of the Competition Appeal Court.[61] He appoints all judges on advice from the JSC and acting judges in consultation with the Chief Justice.[62] The president further appoints heads of many vital public institutions. These include the National Director of Public Prosecutions, the Public Protector,[63] the Auditor-General, members of the South African Human Rights Commission, the Commission for Gender Equality, and the Electoral Commission on recommendation from the National Assembly[64] and may remove[65] members of Chapter 9 institutions on specified grounds. She appoints commissioners of the Public Service Commission,[66] the head of the defence force and the military command of the defence force,[67] the head of the police,[68] the head of the intelligence service[69] and members of the Financial and Fiscal Commission.[70] Under a variety of legislative instruments, the president appoints the Statistician General,[71] the Governor and Deputy Governor of the South African Reserve Bank,[72] the Commissioner of the South African Revenue Service,[73] Members of the Tax Court,[74] and members of the Independent Communications Authority of South Africa.[75] As you would expect, powers of appointment are often coupled with powers of removal, albeit subject to some prescribed process.

The vast powers of appointment of the national executive bring to the fore the debate whether the democratic project will be best served by a powerful central executive authority. Our courts have had to adjudicate challenges against the rationality of several appointments made by the president. It is self-evident that an appointment by a deliberative collective is less vulnerable to a legal challenge of rationality than an appointment by an individual functionary. The ultimate question is how best we may shield appointments of public functionaries to institutions that gird our democracy from the personal preferences and vagary of the appointing authority. The question may be asked differently: how best must we safeguard the effectiveness and integrity of public institutions indispensable to the democratic polity? Finally, an equally important debate should be whether appointing members of the cabinet exclusively from the ranks of members of Parliament best advances the duty members of Parliament have to hold the executive to account. If their career logical advancement is within the national executive, are members of Parliament likely to rattle the executive cage? Will they fulfil their constitutional mandate by holding the national executive to account?

This uncanny concentration of power is a matter that, going forward, we may ignore, but only at our peril.

Trends in Conflict Resolution

Adam Przeworski is a Polish scholar on politics and democracy. He says:

> *Democracy is the realm of the intermediate; the future is not written. Conflicts of values and of interests are inherent in all societies. Democracy is needed precisely because we cannot agree. Democracy is only a system for processing conflicts without killing one another; it is a system in which there are differences, conflicts, winners and losers. Conflicts are absent only in the authoritarian systems.*

Statistics on the number of public protests, some of which tend to be violent, are startling. In the last twelve months, the police reported 11,688 service delivery or other protests in our country.[76] It is fair to consider public protests as a dispute resolution mechanism that is readily available to the working and the marginalised poor people. Some protests yield the desired results and officialdom acts to appease, others not.

A trend not unlike civil protests is the contestation that occurs in the rarefied setting of a court room. Litigation, in our country too, has become a preserve of those who wield public power and purse and those who can pay for it out of available resources. The ever-bulging court roll at the Constitutional Court tends to be dominated by state litigants, followed by business enterprises and labour matters. All three classes of litigants are funded by a collective purse. A trickle of disputes is prosecuted by public interest law firms for vulnerable classes of citizens.

Superior courts of our country are confronted by an avalanche of litigation from powerful interests in the land. This phenomenon is known as *lawfare*. In the past, law has played a very important role in our history. Apartheid oppression was itself a collection of laws that were harnessed to achieve unjust economic and political ends. However, in the eyes of the majority of people there was no rational divide between law and politics. Law served narrow political ends and courts were seen as mere instruments. In the process, their legitimacy suffered and waned. Activists prosecuted spirited political struggles in courts and through the law. Activists, too, used courts and the law to proclaim their cause. This point is made rather sharply by Dennis Davis and Michelle Le Roux in *Precedent and Possibility*.[77] They correctly observe that:

During the long night of apartheid, courts were often sites of vigorous political struggle, being places where different visions of the country were presented to the public by competing litigants, usually the state against accused persons or applicants whose rights were at stake. Since 1994, and the advent of constitutional democracy, similarly significant contests have taken place in the courts. There is however a major difference: Litigation now takes place within the context of the Constitution which provides a vast range of rights for all who live in the country.

Despite the advent of democracy, the tide has shot up. South African courts have, particularly of late, been confronted with a series of challenges that turn on a variety of disputes. Some are essentially of a political nature: the termination of the Scorpions and its replacement by the Hawks;[78] the extension of the term of office of the Chief Justice;[79] the appointment of judges to the Cape High Court;[80] the appointment of the National Director of Public Prosecutions;[81] the challenge into the arms deal which has finally ended with the appointment of a Commission of Enquiry; a parliamentary dispute over a motion of no confidence;[82] the powers of the public protector; and appointment battles within state enterprises. The labour movement itself resorts to the Courts often to resolve internal schism and contestation. Courts adjudicate routinely on disputes arising from state tenders. Indeed, a plethora of business claims land in our courts, whether about collusive trading and price-fixing to tax of forex claims such as those of Mr Shuttleworth and the Reserve Bank.[83] But in the front row of litigation is our democratic state.

This excessive use of the courts speaks to the concern that democratic arrangements in our land are virtually devoid of non-litigious sites for mediation of conflict. Why would party faithful rush off to court to resolve an internecine dispute? Why is the state the chief of all litigators? How does it happen that labour federations should seek solace in court processes? It is not unusual to hear activists or senior politicians vowing to go to the Constitutional Court. Dennis Davis suggests that this trend is 'primarily owing to a manifest failure, perceived or real, of the political process. When politics fail, the last (and often only) avenue left to affected parties is to proceed to court'.[84] The more this trend continues, the more the courts are drawn into the political arena.

But courts are not, and should not be, a substitute for the obligation to move our society to spaces envisioned in the Constitution. We must rethink our democratic processes in a manner that permits peaceable conflict mediation. We must find a new ethos that permits the lamb and the lion to graze together. Losers and winners should both overcome. Like Dennis Davis, allow me to recall Achille Mbembe ('Forward' to *An Inconvenient Youth*) who wrote of the current dangers of South Africa in these terms:

> ... *a gradual closing of life chances for many; an increasing polarisation of the racial structure; a structure of indecision at the heart of politics itself; and a re-balkanisation of culture and society. These trends clearly undermine the fragile forms of mutuality that could have been painstakingly built in South Africa over a decade and a half and further weaken the prospects of true non-racialism ...*

> ... *Stuck in a field of blighted possibilities, [young black youth] scavenge to live or simply to get through the day – so many bad jobs available to so few in one of the most racially unequal countries on Earth; so much rage and almost no future.*

We in the courts are going to continue manning our posts and securing rule of law and justice. But, in the end, a just society envisioned in our Constitution will emerge only from truly democratic and socially inclusive practices of our people.

Concluding Remarks

We have not found a satisfactory solution to spatial apartheid, equitable access to land, and housing and basic services. There is no significant rural development that would have stemmed poverty-stricken urbanisation. The epicentre of economic power is still vested in monopoly capital. Mineral resources in the past and now do not trickle down to workers and the broader populace. Race is still a marker of social inequality. The income disparity has become bigger and starker. Only a small crust of the black middle class has advanced economically against the backdrop of nearly a third of us on social grants and another third of our youth unemployed. We must be disturbed that, up to now, we have not learned how to create jobs for ourselves. After all, a claim to liberty is a claim for space to prosper oneself or community. It is not happening. Instead, poverty is deepening. We have not skilled our children enough to be entrepreneurs and not job hunters. Quality education and health care are still only for the financially healed. I am afraid I must add and confess that proper access to justice is often a function of one's bank balance. We have a lot to do in the next two decades.

Let me seek final refuge in two memorable quotations. Franz Fanon will have the last word:

Each generation must discover its mission, fulfill it or betray it, in relative opacity.
— **Frantz Fanon, *The Wretched of the Earth***

A government or a party gets the people it deserves and sooner or later a people gets the government it deserves.
— **Frantz Fanon, *The Wretched of the Earth***

End Notes

1. *New York Times* article titled '"We the people" loses appeal with people around the world', published 6 February 2012.
2. Published in *New York University Law Review*, Vol. 87, 2012.
3. Professor David Law and Professor Mila Versteeg.
4. At p. 809–29.
5. Section 1 of the Constitution of the Republic of South Africa.
6. Section 23.
7. Section 24.
8. Section 25.
9. Sections 26 and 27.
10. Section 28.
11. Section 29.
12. Section 181–194 of the Constitution.
13. *Bhe and Others v Khayelitsha Magistrate and Others* (CCT 49/03) [2004] ZACC 17; 2005 (1) SA 580 (CC); 2005 (1) BCLR 1 (CC) (15 October 2004); *August and Another v Electoral Commission and Others* (CCT8/99) [1999] ZACC 3; 1999 (3) SA 1; 1999 (4) BCLR 363 (1 April 1999); *Brink v Kitshoff NO* [1996] ZACC 9; 1996 (4) SA 197; 1996 (6) BCLR 752.
14. *Minister of Home Affairs and Another v Fourie and Another* [2005] ZACC 19; 2006 (3) BCLR 355 (CC); 2006 (1) SA 524 (CC); *Larbi-Odam and Others v Member of the Eexecutive Council for Education (North-West Province) and Another* (CCT2/97) [1997] ZACC 16; 1997 (12) BCLR 1655; 1998 (1) SA 745.
15. *Minister of Finance and Other v Van Heerden* [2004] ZACC 3; 2004 (6) SA 121 (CC); 2004 (11) BCLR 1125 (CC); [2004] 12 BLLR 1181 (CC).
16. *Grootboom and Others v Oostenberg Municipality and Others* [1999] ZAWCHC 1 (17 December 1999); *S v Baloyi and Others* (CCT29/99) [1999] ZACC 19; 2000 (1) BCLR 86; 2000 (2) SA 425 (CC); *Somali Association of South Africa and Others v Limpopo Department of Economic Development Environment and Tourism and Others* (48/2014) [2014] ZASCA 143.
17. *Minister of Health and Others v Treatment Action Campaign and Others* (No 2) [2002] ZACC 15; 2002 (5) SA 721; 2002 (10) BCLR 1033.
18. *Government of the Republic of South Africa and Others v Grootboom and Others* [2000] ZACC 19; 2001 (1) SA 46; 2000 (11) BCLR 1169.
19. *Zulu and 389 Others v eThekwini Municipality and Others* [2014] ZACC 17; 2014 (4) SA 590 (CC); 2014 (8) BCLR 971 (CC).
20. *Minister of Public Works and Others v Kyalami Ridge Environmental Association and Others* (Mukhwevho Intervening) [2001] ZACC 19; 2001 (3) SA 1151 (CC); 2001 (7) BCLR 652 (CC).
21. *Occupiers of 51 Olivia Road, Berea Township and 197 Main Street Johannesburg v City of Johannesburg and Others* [2008] ZACC 1; 2008 (3) SA 208 (CC); 2008 (5) BCLR 475 (CC).
22. *City of Johannesburg Metropolitan Municipality v Blue Moonlight Properties 39 (Pty) Ltd*

and Another (CC) [2011] ZACC 33; 2012 (2) BCLR 150 (CC); 2012 (2) SA 104 (CC).

23. *City of Johannesburg and Others v Mazibuko and Others* (489/08) [2009] ZASCA 20; 2009 (3) SA 592 (SCA); 2009 (8) BCLR 791 (SCA); [2009] 3 All SA 202 (SCA).

24. *Head of Department: Mpumalanga Department of Education and Another v Hoërskool Ermelo and Another* [2009] ZACC 32; 2010 (2) SA 415 (CC); 2010 (3) BCLR 177 (CC).

25. *Section 27 and Others v Minister of Education and Another* [2012] ZAGPPHC 114; [2012] 3 All SA 579 (GNP); 2013 (2) BCLR 237 (GNP); 2013 (2) SA 40 (GNP).

26. *Khosa and Others v Minister of Social Development and Others, Mahlaule and Another v Minister of Social Development* [2004] ZACC 11; 2004 (6) SA 505 (CC); 2004 (6) BCLR 569 (CC).

27. *National Education Health & Allied Workers Union (NEHAWU) v University of Cape Town and Others* [2002] ZACC 27; 2003 (2) BCLR 154; 2003 (3) SA 1 (CC); *South African Police Services v Nkambule and Others* [2013] ZALCPE 11.

28. *Laugh It Off Promotions CC v SAB International (Finance) BV t/a Sabmark International (Freedom of Expression Institute as Amicus Curiae)* [2005] ZACC 7, 2006 (1) SA 144 (CC); 2005 (8) BCLR 743 (CC).

29. *Khumalo v Holomisa* [2002] ZACC 12, 2002 (5) SA 401 (CC), 2002 (8) BCLR 771 (CC).

30. *Viking Pony Africa Pumps (Pty) Ltd t/a Tricom Africa v Hidro-Tech Systems (Pty) Ltd and Another* [2010] ZACC 21; 2011 (1) SA 327 (CC); 2011 (2) BCLR 207 (CC).

31. Section 217.

32. *Selebi v S* (240/2011) [2011] ZASCA 249; 2012 (1) SA 487 (SCA); 2012 (1) SACR 209 (SCA); [2012] 1 All SA 332 (SCA).

33. *S v Shaik and Others* [2008] ZACC 7; 2008 (5) SA 354 (CC); 2008 (2) SACR 165 (CC); 2008 (8) BCLR 834 (CC).

34. *Competition Commission v Engen Petroleum Ltd* [2012] ZACT 14; *Competition Commission v Pioneer Foods (Pty) Ltd* [2010] ZACT 9 (Commission imposed unprecedented R1,000,000,000 penalty on Pioneer for collusive price fixing, with respect to bread and flour which undoubtedly harmed the most vulnerable consumers.).

35. Originally published as *Les damnés de la terre* (1961, François Maspero éditeur: Paris).

36. A recent account of this can be found in *We want what's ours: Learning from South Africa's Land Restitution Program* by Professor Bernadette Atuahene (2014, Oxford University Press).

37. Section 25 of the Constitution reads:

(1) No one may be deprived of property except in terms of law of general application, and no law may permit arbitrary deprivation of property.

(2) Property may be expropriated only in terms of law of general application:

(a) for a public purpose or in the public interest; and

(b) subject to compensation, the amount of which, and the time and manner of payment of which, have either been agreed to by those affected or decided or approved by a court.

(3) The amount of the compensation and the time and manner of payment must be just and equitable, reflecting an equitable balance between the public interest and the interests of those affected, having regard to all relevant circumstances, including:

(a) the current use of the property;

(b) the history of the acquisition and use of the property;

(c) the market value of the property;

(d) the extent of direct state investment and subsidy in the acquisition and beneficial capital improvement of the property; and

(e) the purpose of the expropriation.

(4) For the purposes of this section:

(a) the public interest includes the nation's commitment to land reform, and to reforms to bring about equitable access to all of South Africa's natural resources; and

(b) property is not limited to land.

(5) The state must take reasonable legislative and other measures within its available resources to foster conditions which enable citizens to gain access to land on an equitable basis.

(6) A person or community whose tenure of land is legally insecure as a result of past racially discriminatory laws or practices is entitled, to the extent provided by an Act of Parliament, either to tenure which is legally secure or to comparable redress.

(7) A person or community dispossessed of property after 19 June 1913 as a result of past racially discriminatory laws or practices is entitled, to the extent provided by an Act of Parliament, either to restitution of that property or to equitable redress.

(8) No provision of this section may impede the state from taking legislative and other measures to achieve land, water and related reform in order to redress the results of past racial discrimination, provided that any departure from the provisions of this section is in accordance with the provisions of section 36(1).

(9) Parliament must enact the legislation referred to in subsection (6).

38. Section 25(7).

39. Section 25(6).

40. This legislation is the Restitution of Land Rights Act 22 of 1994.

41. Section 25(1).

42. Section 25(3).

43. The most recent Annual Report by the Commission on Restitution of Land Rights, for the review period 1 April 2013–31 March 2014, provides the following information: 'A total of 3.07 million hectares acquired at a cost of R17 billion and financial compensation in the amount of R8 billion has been awarded to 1.8 million beneficiaries coming from 371,140 families of which 138,456 are female-headed families. In addition, R4.1 billion has been awarded to those beneficiaries that have been awarded land as development assistance. The total cost of the restitution programme to date stands at R29.3 billion.'

44. This Annual Report also reflects that to date the Commission on Restitution of Land Rights has settled 77,610 claims.

45. On 1 July 2014, the Restitution of Land Rights Amendment Act 15 of 2014 came into effect, which reopened the restitution claims process that closed at the end of 1998 and gives claimants five years until 30 June 2019 to lodge further claims.

46. *South African National Roads Agency Limited v City of Cape Town and Others; In Re: Protea Parkway Consortium v City of Cape Town and Others* [2014] ZAWCHC 125.

47. See *Zulu* at 19 above.

48. *Pilane and Another v Pilane and Another* [2013] ZACC 3; 2013 (4) BCLR 431 (CC);
    Bengwenyama Minerals (Pty) Ltd and Others v Genorah Resources (Pty) Ltd and Others
    [2010] ZACC 26; 2011 (4) SA 113 (CC); 2011 (3) BCLR 229 (CC).
49. Section 1 of the Constitution.
50. *South Africa Economic Update* – The other eleven middle-income sample countries
    were Armenia, Bolivia, Brazil, Costa Rica, El Salvador, Ethiopia, Guatemala, Indonesia,
    Mexico, Peru and Uruguay. Available online at http://www.worldbank.org/
    content/dam/Worldbank/document/Africa/South%20Africa/Report/south-africa-
    economic-update-2013.05.pdf
51. *South Africa Economic Update.*
52. Section 9.
53. Section 41.
54. Not included in the next paragraph: Section 84 (2)(f) of the Constitution empowers
    the president to appoint commissions of enquiry; Section 93(1)(a) and (b) of the
    Constitution enables the president to appoint any number of deputy ministers from
    among members of the National Assembly and no more than two deputy ministers
    from outside the Assembly to assist the members of the Cabinet, and may also dismiss
    them; Section 178(j) of the Constitution empowers the president to designate four
    persons to the Judicial Service Commission in consultation with the leaders of parties
    in the National Assembly; Section 209(1) empowers the president alone to establish an
    intelligence service other than the defence and police force. Section 6(1) of the
    Electoral Commission Act 51 of 1966 empowers the president to appoint the five
    members of the Electoral Commission one of whom must be a judge; Section 5(2) of
    the Telecommunications Act 13 of 2000 empowers the president to appoint one of the
    councillors as chairperson of the council; Section 22 (4) of the Restitution of Land
    Rights Act 22 of 1994 empowers the president to appoint additional judges to the Land
    Claims Court in consultation with the Judicial Service Commission.
55. Section 91(2) of the Constitution.
56. Section 91(2) and 91(4) of the Constitution.
57. Section 84 (2)(i) of the Constitution.
58. Section 174 (3) of the Constitution.
59. Section 22(3) of the Restitution of Land Rights Act 22 of 1994 as amended by the
    Restitution of Land Rights Act 15 of 2014.
60. Section 26(3) of the Competition Act 89 of 1998.
61. Section 36(2)(a) of the Competition Act 89 of 1998.
62. Sections 174 (4) and (6) and Section 175 of the Constitution.
63. Section 179 (1)(a) of the Constitution.
64. Section 193(4) of the Constitution.
65. Section 194(1) of the Constitution.
66. Section 196 (7) of the Constitution.
67. Section 202 (1) of the Constitution.
68. Section 207(1) of the Constitution.
69. Section 209 (2) of the Constitution.
70. Section 221 of the Constitution.
71. Section 6(1) of the Statistics Act 6 of 1999.

72. Section 4(1)(a) of the South African Reserve Bank Act 90 of 1989.

73. Section 6(1) of the South African Revenue Services Act 34 of 1997.

74. Section 83(5)(a) of the Income Tax Act 58 of 1962.

75. Section 5(1) of the Telecommunications Act 13 of 2000.

76. Available at http://www.saps.gov.za/about/stratframework/annualreports.php

77. Davis and Le Roux. 2009. *Precedent and Possibility – The (Ab)use of Law in South Africa*, p.1. Cape Town: Juta.

78. *Glenister v President of the Republic of South Africa and Others* (CCT 48/10) [2011] ZACC 6; 2011 (3) SA 347 (CC); 2011 (7) BCLR 651 (CC).

79. *Justice Alliance of South Africa v President of Republic of South Africa and Others, Freedom Under Law v President of Republic of South Africa and Others, Centre for Applied Legal Studies and Another v President of Republic of South Africa and Others* (CCT 53/11, CCT 54/11, CCT 62/11) [2011] ZACC 23; 2011 (5) SA 388 (CC); 2011 (10) BCLR 1017 (CC).

80. *Helen Suzman Foundation v Judicial Service Commission and Others* (8647/2013) [2014] ZAWCHC 136.

81. *Democratic Alliance v President of South Africa and Others* (CCT 122/11) [2012] ZACC 24; 2012 (12) BCLR 1297 (CC); 2013 (1) SA 248 (CC).

82. *Mazibuko v Sisulu and Another* (CCT 115/12) [2013] ZACC 28; 2013 (6) SA 249 (CC); 2013 (11) BCLR 1297 (CC).

83. *Shuttleworth v South African Reserve Bank and Others* (864/2013) [2014] ZASCA 157.

84. Supreme Court Judge Dennis Davis. 2011. 'The Judiciary: in the Political Storm?' Talk given to the Cape Town Press Club on 25 November. Speech Transcript: http://www.capetownpc.org.za/

PART 1

REFLECTIONS ON HISTORICAL MOMENTS

South Africa arrived at the political transition and ultimately democracy twenty years ago through intensive struggle in various forms, and through a range of talks and negotiations. There were key moments, prior to 1994, which brought about the first democratic elections on 27 April 1994. This section on Reflections on Historical Moments provides consideration of the historical nodal points that led to democracy in South Africa. In view of the current realities in the socio-economic spheres, there are pertinent questions that people are asking as to the nature of the negotiations, the determinant forces and the compromises reached. Issues such as the paths chosen for economic development, reconciliation and the building of the state are aired here.

REFLECTIONS ON HISTORICAL MOMENTS – FRENE GINWALA

There were no instant victories or 'Eureka Moments' that marked the outcome of negotiations and the nature and content of our democracy. Rather, there were intensive struggles in the face of increasing violence and repression to bring about any form of dialogue and eventually negotiations.

Post World War II British colonies gradually won their independence through negotiations. For South Africa, in 1910 the British Parliament enacted a constitution that disenfranchised the majority of the population and handed political power to white South Africans alone. This power was used to further dispossess the African people of their land and subjugate the majority of the population with force.

In 1948, the victory of the National Party led to the imposition of ever harsher racist policies through greater repression and violence. Resistance shifted from making representations to mass action, with growing unity within the black population. The 1950s opened with widespread civil disobedience campaigns. The government response was deportations and banishment to rural areas, detentions and the banning of leaders. As individual leaders were banned, new ones were elected in an acting capacity as the population refused to allow the government to choose their leaders. In many of the organisations there were acting-acting-acting secretary-generals and so on, while resistance continued.

ANC leaders, convinced that the organisation would eventually be banned, decided that an external mission would need to be established to speak on behalf of the oppressed. Historically, the political head of the ANC was the president-general. At its 1952 conference, the ANC appointed a committee chaired by Oliver Tambo to review its constitution. The 1958 conference adopted the new constitution, which, for the first time, provided for a deputy president. The conference elected Oliver Tambo (who had been previously identified to leave the country) as that deputy president.

The Sharpeville Massacre of 1960 precipitated events. The National Executive Committee (NEC) of the ANC met in Cape Town and decided Oliver Tambo should leave the country immediately and proceed with the plan to establish the external mission, which would become the voice of the oppressed majority. Confirmation had been received from Julius Nyerere that, though Tanganyika was not yet fully independent, any ANC leaders who reached the country would not be returned to South Africa. Reassured, Oliver Tambo and Dr Yusuf Dadoo (former President of the South African Indian Congress) proceeded to Dar es Salaam and began their work.

Inside the country, Umkhonto we Sizwe (MK) launched the armed struggle. Later, Nelson Mandela left the country clandestinely and, together with Oliver Tambo, visited a number of African countries. Mandela received military training and arranged for training facilities in a number of African and other countries. Acts of sabotage followed. MK attempted to re-enter South Africa through Zimbabwe and Botswana.

The apartheid regime was still considered as an ally of the Western world in its battle against communism. However, this was not the view of their populations. Together with the ANC, the people of these countries mobilised to put pressure on their own governments to change their policies: organising sports, cultural and academic boycotts and forming anti-apartheid movements. South Africa was excluded from the Olympics; there were calls for sanctions and trade boycotts and an arms embargo. Following the revolution in Iran, South Africa lost its guaranteed oil supply. A special unit to stop oil reaching South Africa by covert means succeeded in identifying the source of 80 to 90 per cent of the oil reaching South Africa. India had already imposed sanctions. Sweden stopped investment in South Africa. Norway stopped its oil being sold to South Africa and also its tankers carrying any oil to South Africa.

The major impact was made by financial sanctions, organised through an *End Loans to South Africa* campaign. There was pressure on local and international banks to disengage from South Africa. Finally, some major US and British banks, faced with local boycotts, did so. The financial sanctions affected the South African regime, particularly at a time when it was trying to buy support from the African people by talk of reform and upgrading some of the townships. But additional expenditure affected the regime's ability to continue to buy support from the white population.

White South Africans started to make contact with the liberation movement. Some came to assess what 'these demons' were like, some out of concern for their future and for their investments – lawyers, students, business leaders, judges, faith leaders, professional bodies, etc. Each group came seeking reassurance for its own interests, but many also came out of genuine concern for the future of the country.

The dialogue had begun and took many forms. The ANC produced constitutional guidelines for a democratic South Africa that were discussed by the membership and later with visiting delegations and democratic organisations in the country. Gradually, these meetings became more than 'getting to know you' exercises. The Pretoria regime monitored these informal talks, but also tried to intervene as it did with the judges, and more drastically with a member of the South African Parliament. The US Ambassador in Lusaka set up breakfast meetings with individuals or groups from South Africa. There were also 'feelers' coming from semi-official bodies and envoys suggesting meetings with senior ANC leaders. These were not rejected and 'talks about talks' took place.

The ANC continued to make its own plans. We issued policy papers and conferences were held. The post-apartheid research group accessed research from inside South Africa and arranged 'academic' meetings. Secret, unofficial 'exploratory' talks began, aimed at identifying common ground. The regime began contact with Nelson Mandela, initially to assess what sort of person he was. At the same time, Pretoria continued its attacks on ANC personnel, sending death squads into neighbouring countries and invading Angola.

In the 1980s, the ANC published material, including official secret documents, revealing that the apartheid regime had acquired nuclear technology and was building nuclear weapons. Western countries and companies assisting the regime were identified. This added pressure on the apartheid regime and the countries supporting it.

The purpose of this brief history is to illustrate that the apartheid regime came to negotiations from a position of weakness. It had run out of options and there was no way it could reverse the process. As it lost its international support and failed to eliminate people's resistance and destroy their organisations, it gradually released senior leaders who were in prison, and eventually unbanned the ANC and announced the release of Nelson Mandela. The question we need to ask is: in these circumstances, to what extent did we take advantage of their weakness?

The process of negotiations is well known. I need, however, to stress that many of the claims of concessions that were made are incorrect. The National Party was unable to secure group rights in the constitution. Its desire for a constitutionally enforced coalition government also failed when it was unable to establish that the Swiss constitution provided for this. Also, the allegations that the 'concessions' allegedly made on land have prevented the restitution of land are not true. Our Constitution does not preclude the acquisition of land in the national interest. This has been done in many countries including the United States. I need not elaborate on this, as the previous speaker, Deputy Chief Justice Dikgang Moseneke, has explained more authoritatively than I ever could.

In 1988, at an ANC women's conference attended by a number of MK commanders, there were detailed discussions and programmes. A pledge made by President Tambo at a press conference before the UN Womens' Conference in Nairobi, that South Africa could never be truly free until the women of South Africa were fully liberated, was confirmed. This commitment is reflected in the values of our democratic constitution: that non-racialism and non-sexism shall be the founding provisions of a new constitution for the democratic South Africa.

The same ANC conference called for a new Women's Charter to be drafted by all South African women. After the unbanning of the ANC, a Women's National Coalition, including all women's organisations, was formed. After an extensive consultation process, the Coalition agreed on 'The Women's Charter for Effective Equality.' Copies were presented to the Speaker of the National Assembly and the Chairperson of the Constitutional Assembly, now Deputy President of democratic South Africa.

Yet, in this twentieth year of our democracy we find growing violence against women and girl children. Women are amongst the lowest paid workers. They are the poorest of the poor, and in their old age need to continue to care for their grandchildren. The challenge remains as to how we are dealing with this. How can we justify the poverty, the terrible living conditions, the lack of clean water and sanitation and electricity and the crime and gratuitous violence against children and young and old women?

In the first two years of our democratic Parliament, we began the process of addressing the status and condition of women in the national budget. But that has fallen by the wayside. Today we speak of the National Development Plan, but where and how are the issues concerning women reflected?

I would like to quote part of Article 3 of the 'Women's Charter for Effective Equality':

> Women claim involvement in decision making and full participation at all levels and in all aspects of the formal and _informal economy_. All definitions of economic activity such as those used in the national accounts must be expanded to specify informal sector and subsistence activities and must include all forms of unpaid labour.

Currently, the issue of a national minimum wage is being debated. This provides an opportunity to review the historic low wage levels for the jobs and professions in which women dominate. The call for 'Equal Pay for Work of Equal Value' was first made by the President of the Bantu Women's League, Charlotte Maxeke, at the Conference of the Industrial and Commercial Workers' Union (ICU) in the 1920s. In countries where this principle has been implemented, women's wages have increased by up to 30 per cent and the subsistence economy is reflected in the national accounts. Is this not an option for the way forward in our democracy?

Is not the best option to seize the opportunity of a national minimum wage? It is not a women's issue. It is an issue of subsistence farmers, of farm workers, domestic workers, nurses as well. It requires rethinking our notion of economic development.

A society that permits sexism and patriarchy to prevail cannot claim to be a true democracy.

REFLECTIONS ON HISTORICAL MOMENTS – SYDNEY MUFAMADI

Allow me to start off with a commercial. You know, a friend of mine, a very close comrade, Aziz Pahad, launched a book recently. It's called *The Insurgent Diplomat*. I happened to have attended the launch of the book, and present at the launch were people who spanned four generations of pro-democracy activists. Well, Comrade Frene and myself do not belong quite to the same generation so I speak in this connection of the pre-Morogoro generation, the post-Morogoro generation, the 76 *klip gooiers*, the 1980s and the post-1990 generation.

But I think it's important when we talk about these generations not to rely on a clinical forensic audit in order to determine the delineation between these generations, otherwise we will lose sight of the reality that there is a porosity of boundaries between these generations. For instance, I said Comrade Frene and myself do not belong to the same generation, but there is a sense in which we belong to the same generation. So I'm saying that these are not necessarily clinically delineated.

Now I am being asked here to talk about a reflection on historical moments. I thought it necessary to point out from the outset that an identification thereof tends to depend on where you sat at different stages of the evolution of the struggle for change.

Now, coming back to the book by Aziz – which I recommend very much to people who are interested in this topic that we are discussing – when you go through it you will find that it spotlights a period that does not feature very much in public discourse, because that is the period during which there were secret talks leading up to the Convention for a Democratic South Africa (Codesa). It was really a period during which the movement was groping for stones under feet in order to establish the possibility of crossing the river. So, in as much as those were secret talks, they served as the legwork that was necessary in order to set the scene for the great inclusive national dialogue that came to be known as Codesa.

Now, from my vantage point, I happen to have been part of a mass democratic movement, and I must hasten to point out that, although the ANC was illegal, the ANC was strongly tethered to this dynamic mass democratic movement, which partly explains why, as Comrade Frene was saying, the other side came to the negotiating table from a position of weakness. Let me say, in order to bring a little bit of context to this, those of us who were in the leadership of the mass democratic movement more or less at the same time as these secret talks that Aziz talks about were taking place in London and elsewhere, were also involved in discussions with representatives of the 'other side', but with many of the people who were responsible for rationalising historically the system that we were fighting against. And their interest in discussing with us, in the same way as the interests of the people who were discussing with the ANC in London, was non-trivial. It was an indication at the time that some of them had actually lost confidence in the permanence of the system which they had been rationalising for so many years.

So if you look at the negotiating concept of the ANC, the Harare Declaration, you will see a sentence that turns around a very difficult word that only the Judge can explain. It says 'there exists in our country a conjecture of circumstances which makes a negotiated settlement possible'. That was a diagnosis of the balance of forces as we saw them at the time. In other words, we understood that this behaviour by the Afrikaner elite was just an epiphenomenon of a movement which needed to be assimilated into a programme: our own programme of hegemonic interpolation. In other words, it was becoming clear to us that the 'other side' was resigning itself to the inevitability of change and, therefore, in the circumstances, the task that was facing us was to ensure that we didn't allow them to hegemonise that process of change. It ties in with the point that Dr Ginwala was making: they came to the negotiating table with clearly defined objectives – group rights and other objectives – that they sought to achieve, and we had to be vigilant about them.

Again, if you look at the Harare Declaration, you will see a section there, a statement of principles. That section (it's important to say this) was not in the original draft on the basis of which Oliver Tambo at the time moved around the region consulting with the African leadership about our negotiating concept. It came in after an important observation was made by then-President of Tanzania, Julius Nyerere. He said you must use this opportunity not just to go and negotiate but to reach out to the generality of the South African population, including the people that the apartheid regime believes it represents. He said, as I understand it, your vision for a new South Africa is eminently reasonable. It is necessary, therefore, for you to try and tackle the other side's years of strategic instrumentalisation of deception, the things they used to say about the ANC and the rest of the liberation movement. You need to use your own negotiating concept to engage in dialogue with the people who have fallen for what the other side had been doing for years. They created their own ANC. They believed in what they had created. Nyerere made the point that it is important to drive home this message that there is a difference between the real ANC and this putative ANC that was created by the other side for obvious reasons.

That brings me to one of the events I regard as one of the important nodal points in the movement from where we were at the time up to 1994. I'm talking about an event at which, if he hasn't forgotten, our keynote speaker, Judge Dikgang Moseneke, was present. Do you remember that, sir? You are not under oath. I happened to have attended that Frontline Heads of State Summit in Harare in 1992, carrying Walter Sisulu's briefcase to the summit because he was representing the African National Congress. It was a special summit that was called in the immediate aftermath of the White's-only referendum – you remember that – and the leaders in the frontline states were interested to understand, now that the referendum had happened, whereto from here?

And submissions were called for from the ANC and the PAC because those were accredited liberation movements of the time. I'm going to say a few things, mindful of the fact that protocol does not allow me to reclaim the Deputy Chief Justice as one of our own, but I am talking about him in his previous incarnation as Comrade Dikgang Moseneke. Walter Sisulu said to that summit: 'In principle we were opposed to this referendum and we said so publicly; however, we said, despite our opposition to it, we call on the whites, should they decide to participate in it, to vote in favour of a negotiating process because De Klerk was saying "I need a mandate on whether to negotiate or not". And some were saying: 'But it can't be just the whites who decide this question.' So he said, 'Well, we are happy that the majority of the whites voted in favour of this negotiations process, therefore De Klerk has no excuse.' The PAC position, which was well articulated then by its vice-president who was leading the PAC delegation, was that the referendum was a non-event and we were asking you to pay no attention to the outcome of that referendum. The struggle continues, asking for all-round support to mount the revolution to its logical conclusion.

It was interesting to see what kind of advice came from those heads of state. I remember one of them saying: 'You know, you are the liberation movement; your mission has always been about bringing about change in South Africa; now, if the majority of the whites have voted in favour of a movement towards a new South Africa, however they define this change, it must mean that they are coming closer to embracing this cause for which you have always been fighting.' I think we were being advised to understand and relate to the change process in its dialectical complexity. And I think we gained a lot from the advice that we were given. You can see now, as we speak, that we speak with the benefit of hindsight and a bit of wisdom, even when we talk about where we came from and where are we now.

Let me then try to say, twenty years of democracy, where to now? But, by way of transition into this part of my input, let me say this: we are now in this new democratic South Africa; we face many challenges. What is critically important for us, given what was said by the earlier speakers and what I have just said, is always to make sure that we understand these challenges in the proper context. The democratic state that we have is based on a vision that is well articulated in the Constitution. We had, before 1994, a national discourse that took various forms – secret talks, an all-inclusive transparent process of negotiations at the World Trade Centre.

When we face challenges today, as we did before, shouldn't we take a leaf from the way we approached our challenges in the past, which is not to allow such problems as we face to paralyse us. Approach them in the same way as we did before. Questions are being raised. Is the momentum of democratic change stalling? There are many things that we see in society which may suggest that it is indeed stalling: the reassertion of ethnic consciousness, the inability on our part sometimes to manage differences amongst ourselves. The example of what is happening in the Congress of South African Trade Unions (Cosatu) was cited. It's not limited to what is happening in the trade union movement. The value of ongoing discourse, consciously organised by ourselves, lies in that it also helps us to overcome the legacy of our own socialisation. Brought up as I was in the liberation movement, there was a time when we used to say we are the sole and authentic representatives of the people. That means that we had no obligation to negotiate with those we believed were there to undermine the agenda of emancipation.

You can see inflections of this thinking in the way, for instance, the current generation of trade union leaders are handling differences amongst themselves – the tendency to move towards excluding those who hold dissenting views. So I am saying that, given the obvious discrepancy between what we had as our guiding vision and what we see happening on the ground every day, it's critically important that, not only should we just talk about what we see, but we fall back to the experience of how we got to where we are. Because, as I say, that will provide us with the material to understand that, through dialogue amongst ourselves, we are even able to handle difficult issues, not only issues that were in any case settled, such as the colour of our national flag and so on.

Discussion focused earlier on issues such as distributional conflicts. How do we handle this? What is our mental model of our national economy and ourselves as a society? South Africa is not a mono-racial society. That history matters in our discussion about the present: how to handle the current problems and how to build consensus amongst ourselves. What is the new force of gravity on which we are going to anchor the new consensus on the basis of which we should move forward as a society? So there is a continuing need for a search for a new basis from which we are going to agree or develop a consensus as to how we move forward to the pinnacle of this democracy, which appears in many ways to be still very elusive.

Beyond the Compromise: Crafting new Visions and Practices of Freedom – Patricia McFadden

Let me pose a few questions as stepping stones into a terrain that is littered with quagmires as well as possibilities; with explanations on how we can make the shift into a different future. Why do we recount (or retell) the past and on whose behalf do these remembrances function? Hopefully, I will make a contribution towards demystifying some of the fictions that have been referred to in the course of my presentation. Is it, then, a telling of 'our story' as a collective/common story or has the past been massaged and re-tailored to fit the particular contours of a current status quo that remains persistently capitalist and feudal – a toxic mixture of inequality, impunity, intolerance and outright arrogance in many instances?

If we can face ourselves and honestly claim that we are retracing the landmarks of our struggles so as to throw open new vistas of a just and dignified future for all, then we can also ask ourselves just how truthfully we have translated the experiences, courage and dreams of those who came before us, who left us along the way to this place of unbridled anger, frustration and unfulfilled expectations for the majority of African people. Only then can we honestly say that we are striving to make freedom for all a reality of our time.

When a society and continent is endowed with enormous wealth – in its people, its natural resources, its languages and cultural treasures – then the bar is set much higher for those who assume a custodial role on behalf of everyone. In this context, 'at least' does not apply. Excellence and the maximum fulfilment of human entitlements are the criteria by which those who occupy the state and control the wealth of the society are assessed and judged, and there can be no excuses. Two decades is a long time in the life of a people who have given countless lives for an ideal; two decades translates into many generations in the lives of working people whose dreams and children provided the grist for the wheels of movement towards freedom as a life of dignity.

This moment offers many opportunities to speak truth to power. I would like to thank the organisers for the honour of the time to share my experiences and ideas as a fighter for freedom, within a community that represents a vital cutting edge in this and all African societies – continentally and across the African Diaspora.

I want to speak to two issues that have preoccupied radical thinkers and activists for many decades on this continent and beyond. These are: the matter of the state and the ruling classes who occupy it and use it to plunder and enrich themselves, even as they proclaim an innocence of economic and other forms of impunity; and the other is the urgency of imagining and launching new social movements that reflect and articulate the key elements of contemporarity – an essential understanding of how we can become contemporary Africans in the context of our particular nationalist historical past; of the critical discourses, resistances and engagements with colonial/capitalist oppression and exploitation; the crafting of radical traditions and practices of imagining, fighting for and defending freedom; and the ability to continuously move forward towards societies that are premised on justice, human integrity and dignity for all citizens.

Neocolonialism – which is the moment in African history when 'the great compromise' is committed by those who claimed to be the custodians of a different future for us all – is a moment that usurps the bravery and dedication of millions of Africans across this continent. This usurpation is performed on behalf of a tiny clique of people who have 'empty hearts', and who treat the common wealth of our societies as though it were their birthright, throwing crumbs at the working people for which they are expected to be grateful. While the primitive accumulation of black ruling classes is moralistically decried as 'corruption' – we understand that to rule in class societies, those who occupy the state must own property – productive and financial property. To rant against the emergence of a black ruling class is to distract attention from a necessary class analysis which enables a clearer understanding of the present and the past.

The moment of neocolonialism, which has spanned half an African century, has become the insignia of the black ruling classes. The adoption of neoliberal capitalist pacts, and the re-institutionalisation of feudal structures and practices as 'culture', have recreated the divide between the working people and state occupants, a divide that was temporarily breached by the fleeting hope that Africa would shift its trajectory away from the colonial infrastructure and its exclusionary practices of racist and classist inequality. Into this divide have rushed the new carpetbaggers of the late twentieth century/early twenty-first century – extremist fundamentalists of both Judeo-Christian and Islamic religious bent, each touting viciously reactionary feudal texts that seek to capture the hearts and minds (and souls) of Africans across the expanse of this continent. And Nationalism seems impotent (pun intended) in the face of this onslaught as we have witnessed all around us.

South Africa represents the most dramatic and most blatant of all the cases we have witnessed on the continent. Neocolonialism was ushered in at the moment of independence with globalised pomp and fanfare – so loud and insistent that it was exceptional and different; the rest of us were astounded at the absurdity of it all. We were, and continue to be, deeply saddened by the enormity of the lost opportunities that South Africa, in all its meanings and possibilities, represented to virtually every black person on this planet.

As the neocolonial crisis deepens, which is inevitable, given that it is built into peripheral capitalism as the backyard of the established Western capitalist system, and the people increasingly occupy the streets and public spaces of the society, demanding their entitlements as the people of this land – yes, entitlement as a consciousness that drives the ability to struggle for rights and dignity as outcomes of contestation and engagement with those who occupy and use the state for their narrow interests – so also the new opportunities for envisioning a different society emerge. We need a new and gender inclusive ideology of national and pan-African nationhood and African identity in all its possibilities – inclusive beyond the mere rhetoric of 'gender mainstreaming'. We need a contemporary imaginary that can be translated into different policies and practices about the land, human sufficiency in all respects, and equitable resource utilisation (or simply the preservation of these resources for future generations of Africans. We cannot allow the ruling classes to recklessly consume the futures of our children and the generations to come through a deceptive ploy such as the 'Africa Rising' rhetoric).

Now that we know the terrain after two decades of lived neocolonialism, the unavoidable question remains – What is to be done? – to retrieve Lenin's call once again.

I think that it is at the intersection of the clash between those who represent the interests of capital and imperial systems of privilege and those who struggle for an equitable distribution of the common wealth of this and all African societies, that the new nodes of an alternative future lie. New notions and vehicles of resistance and progress will have to be imagined, crafted and set into motion among all communities and constituencies of people who are situated outside the state. And engagement on the entitlement to lives of dignity for all in our societies will have to take place in whatever form necessary to make the essential shift from the iniquitous neocolonial/neoliberal capitalist system to the truly inclusive alternative social formations that await this society and the entire continent and the world beyond it.

Whether the shift is sparked off by the refusal of radical trade unions to be erased by compromised alliances that served a conjunctural political purpose that they have long outlived; or lit by the courage of radical intellectuals who refuse to be cowed and silenced by a revisionist telling of our struggles for Freedom and Dignity; or by those of us who already live on the other side of the social curve – embracing the future even as the rest of society grapples with the imperative of having to change; all these, and many more nodes of newness and visionary insight and outsight, are the spokes in the wheels that will take us into the future. The future awaits us. Let us retrieve our courage, embrace it, do what we know has to be done, and make the transformation a reality.

PART 2

THE SOUTH AFRICAN POLITICAL ECONOMY

Over the past twenty years, South Africa's political economy has been defined by the paradox of periods of relatively robust economic growth, stagnation and near recession. Combined with these is the slow pace of job creation, as well as the challenges of poverty and inequality. The National Development Plan (NDP) articulates a vision for the country and the path towards a truly democratic, non-racial, non-sexist, prosperous and equitable society; and it enjoys the support of most sectors of society. However, three related questions deserve interrogation: is the vision appropriate and adequate; is there capacity and will to implement it; and what are the implications of pedestrian economic performance going forward? In brief, where will South Africa be in another twenty years?

THE SOUTH AFRICAN POLITICAL ECONOMY – MIRIAM ALTMAN

The theme of this conference is *20 Years of South African Democracy: So Where to Now?* I was asked to reflect on how the National Development Plan acts as a guide, especially in relation to inclusive growth.

The Plan was meant to offer a vision: one that could draw together all sections of society toward transformative and progressive action. But a lot of misinformation about what the Plan says, has been used to divide society instead. I believe there are a lot of good ideas in the Plan and so did all of Cabinet, every party in parliament and large cross-sections of society. We will make most progress if we focus on having practical debates about how to move forward.

When the Commission started visualising 2030, we asked: 'What kind of economy do we want to have?' and 'What's in the realm of the possible?' and 'How do we start dreaming about what kind of country we want to have?' So one of the proposals was to envisage South Africa as a developed country by 2030. But I felt I would be really happy if we were truly a middle-income country, which means that the majority of the population feels like and experiences what it is to live in a middle-income country. The majority would have access to good schooling, a healthy life – that they're not going to die young – there is a high probability of working, even if it's a low-level job, there is access to public transport, and that prices enable low-income families access to basic goods.

Now, the majority of South Africans don't live that way. We know that – and this is where probably a lot of the frustration of the earlier speakers is – middle-income in Africa is more like the idea of a few rich people and a lot of really poor people. The GDP per capita average is a very abstract idea because middle-income countries in Africa are generally what we would think of as low income. But they have oil, like Nigeria, or minerals, like the DRC, and these exports artificially raise the level of GDP to appear as though they are more developed than they really are. The DRC is a middle-income country. I don't think any of us would think of it as one, but it is. Angola and Botswana are middle-income countries. Now that's not usual, globally, but it is true in Africa where there are great concentrations of wealth and widespread poverty. The GDP per capita is measured as middle income, but the earnings are very poorly distributed. And I think that's where a lot of the expression of frustration comes from this morning.

In South Africa, we have had much debate about Nigeria surpassing us when their GDP was rebased. Ghana is doing the same. Now they are bigger than us. Much was written in the press locally with consternation. But actually, as growth in Nigeria powered ahead – between 2000 and 2011 per capita GDP doubled – the per cent of the population living on less than $1 per day rose by about 12 per cent.

At the other extreme, Korea deeply corrected its development path from the 1970s with consistent long-term commitment to policies that enabled it to power ahead, from industrial policy to significant investments in national education. The statistics show that deep poverty is largely eradicated in Korea.

South Africa's GDP per capita has stagnated, growing by only 22% between 1990 and 2013, from $9,900 to $12,100 (this is measured in purchasing power parity, constant 2005 international dollars, and is sourced from the World Bank). So measured, our GDP per capita in 1990 was similar to that in Korea, Malaysia and Mexico. But by 2013, GDP per capita almost tripled in Korea, from about $12,000 to $32,700. Similarly, Malaysia's GDP per capita more than doubled from about $10,100 to $22,500. Malaysia's poverty headcount fell from about 37 per cent in 1980 to 16 per cent in 1999 to 1.7 per cent in 2012. India's GDP per capita tripled from $1,800 to $5,400, and it halved the per cent of the population living below its poverty line from about 45 per cent in 1994 to 22 per cent in 2012. Mexico raised its GDP per capita by only 30 per cent with no impact in reducing the approximately 52 per cent of the population living below the poverty line.

There is no doubt that economies need to grow to solve big poverty gaps. But the challenge we need to discuss is how the growth is achieved, how the benefits are distributed and what is being done to strengthen institutions.

With this in mind, we put together a range of scenarios to 2030 focused on employment outcomes, looking at certain policy assumptions that different growth rates would be predicated on.

We have faced many who believe that a focus on economic growth means we don't care about people. The idea that one might be completely focused on growth alone is an old one. Perhaps that was the thinking of mainstream economists in the 1950s and 60s. And it is true that a 'trickle down' approach was a dominant view even to the 1990s. The push back on a growth focus is the concern that it has nothing to do with people and only benefits capital. Indeed, there are different approaches and ideologies in respect of how to create employment and stimulate growth. Ultimately, they will rest on the design and strength of institutions, the manner in which business is stimulated, the access that the population has to opportunity, and improving welfare of the population.

The way you get growth in a country like South Africa is to solve the energy constraints, ensure there is sufficient water, promote industry and promote education and training. You make sure that your population is healthy. Sustainable growth depends on people. Those things are fundamentally intertwined and that's what the Plan says. If you read the economy chapter, it starts with a statement that says essentially that these two things are intertwined – to achieve sustainable growth it will have to be inclusive. We could accelerate for short periods by, say, promoting smelter investments, but this will not underpin the long-term improvements we need to dramatically reduce unemployment and poverty.

South Africa needs to grow in a way that creates jobs and enables a decent standard of living. This has four legs: that there is sufficient opportunity so that there is a high probability of working; that the cost of living is affordable and accessible; that there is an enabling system of social protection; and that citizens have a voice in matters affecting their lives.

The challenge now is that we are not really squaring those four and the experience of alienation and marginalisation is coming to the fore. The channels aren't working and people don't feel like they can influence their lives. There is no doubt that we've made major inroads into social services, social grants and so on. But the fact is that the outcomes aren't making sufficient change in the quality of living for the majority, while small sections of society are becoming wealthier. In other words, the unemployment rate is what it was a decade ago, child health and nutrition are still very poor – there is still much to do on many fronts.

In the Plan, we produced three scenarios. Scenario 1 is called 'mediocre minerals', which means we don't break out of our resource curse challenges. In this scenario, we grow by three per cent annually over twenty years. It's a bit more in some years; a bit less in other years. That's essentially the track that we've been on for a very long time. And the reality is that, if we continue on that path, we'll end up with unemployment at around 27 per cent by 2020.

What the Plan is really saying is: we must avoid that path. It is a very real possibility because that is actually the path we're on right now. Not just because we are doing badly this year and our growth rate was downgraded but, as the National Planning Commission, we have to think what might happen over a decade or two. So I am not just looking at the last quarter or the last year. We are on that low-level trajectory and will continue as such if we persist in making decisions as we are and have been. I am speaking about a very long trajectory. We had some per capita GDP growth in the 1960s, which was very poorly distributed and promoting of capital intensity, and a second spurt in the 2000s, but overall our real GDP per capita is now only ten per cent higher than it was in 1980.

We have to break away from this trajectory. We had two short periods of growth over the past five decades. Many countries accelerate like that, but very few sustain. There are maybe thirteen countries globally that have managed to grow for a sustained period such that they break out of their poverty cycle, but very few countries do it. It requires huge commitment.

Now what are some of the external forces we are facing? The first is that, after a long commodity boom, there's slow global growth, and it looks set to be like that for a while. And we are deeply affected by global phenomena as a small open economy. That's a very common challenge faced by many African countries.

We are a minerals economy, and we have to understand that there are common characteristics to countries that sell oil, in particular, and that sell minerals. They tend to have higher inequality than most. They tend to have lower growth. They tend to be less stable. And that's partly due to the economics of a boom and bust cycle and it's also to do with the politics of it. One challenge is related to where the rents and profits accrue from these earnings. But also, the policymakers become lulled into thinking that things are fine during commodity booms. That's exactly what happened in South Africa during the commodity boom. Not that we took full advantage of that commodity boom as we should have. But even then, as we were growing jobs and as the economy was booming, we weren't expanding our manufacturing sector in the way that we should have been, and our high-value services sector.

Policymakers can be fooled by what they see in the domestic economy during a commodity boom. The economy expands, domestic activity is stimulated and jobs are created. The economic statistics that make it appear that you are moving ahead in fact are working against your ability to expand small businesses and manufacturing. The exchange rate appreciates, imports become cheaper, the retail sector is stimulated and manufacturing exports are discouraged. When the commodity boom ends, it all crashes. And that's exactly what's happened in South Africa.

Inequality has been rising in many countries since the late 1980s. A growing share of income accrues to the top ten per cent of income earners and a falling share of income accrues to labour. This is partly due to a falling proportion of jobs in goods production as a result of technology diffusion, and a rising share of services that create both high skill and low wage employment, but limited opportunity in the middle. These are forces we were all facing. But South Africa starts with extremely high levels of inequality. This makes our job of reducing inequality and poverty even more challenging.

Now what do we need to do? What does the Plan say? These are practical elements that we really need to engage with that are within our power to influence.

The first is the infrastructure gaps that stop us in our tracks. We all know we have this energy problem. If you don't have energy you don't just stop the mines, you stop any major property development. Some of the biggest users of energy are in accommodation – hotels, that kind of thing. No big property can be approved unless you can guarantee long-term energy security for it. This will pose a brake on urban development also, where most jobs are created. So it fundamentally shrinks your ability to expand. That is within our power to fix.

Second, we need to stimulate new industries and activities that have the following qualities: they reflect our competitive advantage; there's global growth potential; they can create jobs or they might create jobs indirectly through linkages. Promoting smelting was not an example of that, and fortunately we are not doing that any more. But our emphasis on smelting in the 1990s drew resources from other parts of the economy and put them into a sector that has none of these characteristics. That was a significant policy error of the time.

We need to widen our attention across manufacturing and services sectors. A lot of people were upset that we promoted services sectors in the Plan. Some took that to mean the Plan was not supportive of manufacturing. Quite the opposite is true – we believe that manufacturing is a critical sector, and we make recommendations for focused interventions. However, we do not believe that it will be a major creator of jobs. This is the evidence globally – that the vast majority of jobs are created in services and not in manufacturing. This poses a challenge for the reasons stated earlier – that service jobs tend to be precarious and low paid or, alternatively, high skilled. We applied our minds to approaches that could raise the proportion of service jobs that might be created in better sections of the services sector that could have the properties described earlier: that they are in growing demand globally; that we have competitive advantage; that they could stimulate linkages. This strategy has been pursued by Korea, Malaysia, India, Turkey and a number of successful East European economies, amongst others. We need to locate such growth sectors like IT-enabled services, an industry where India has created two and a half million jobs between 2000 and 2010, with substantial diversification in value-adding activities.

We need to stabilise labour relations. We know that. And it is within our power to do so. We need to strengthen collective bargaining and dispute resolution institutions. We need to ensure compliance to minimums. We talked about minimum wages. Actually, there are minimum wages in any sector you can think of. They just aren't applied. We talked about that in the Plan. We need to introduce much more forceful active labour market policies. We need to strengthen education standards. We make a whole range of recommendations around this. Most importantly, we need to rebalance the cost of living and the quality of living so that your average person, no matter where they are in the socio-economic ladder, can expect their child to go to school, obtain a quality education, finish school, get a bursary, study and bring the family out of poverty.

Right now in South Africa, a very small percentage of the population, less than ten per cent, can even think about that dream, which should be a basic minimum to support our growth path but also to achieving a basic human and decent standard of living.

THE SOUTH AFRICAN POLITICAL ECONOMY – **RENOSI MOKATE**

In my talk I am going to deal with the three or four questions that we were asked to look at on this panel. The first question was to look at the NDP, the National Development Plan 2030, the vision – is it appropriate and adequate? Secondly, is there the capacity and the will to implement it? What are the implications of South Africa's pedestrian economic performance going forward? And what are the challenges and how do we achieve appropriate socio-economic development going forward?

I will try to answer the last two questions as well as I can, given the fact that it is a much more forward-looking sort of approach. With respect to the vision of the NDP and whether or not it's appropriate and adequate, my take on the NDP is that, if you look at the vision, it is aspirational, which I think is a good thing. It tells us about how we all seek a better future for our children and for ourselves. It's inspirational in the sense that it speaks about our future being our responsibility: as the title indicates 'our future, our work'. It's grounded in an understanding of South Africa's social, economic and political conditions as well as its historical contexts.

You will recall that, before the Plan was actually developed, there was a diagnostic done of what the challenges are and, then, based on the evidence, the plan was developed. So in my view, it is very much about South Africa seeking its own answers to the challenges that it faces. And it tries to address all the segments of society. It addresses the individual context by talking about enhancing capabilities and it proposes active citizenship, or agency and voice, as Miriam Altman has indicated. And then, of course, it alludes to the importance of state action through a capable state.

It is also very comprehensive with the many chapters covering the economic, institutional, social and political dimensions, as well as South Africa's position in the world, amongst others. It is pitched at a high level, implying that there is a need for the different sectors of society to give concrete expression to the aspirations that are outlined in the Plan. And it identifies actions for all sectors of society and it does have a significant focus on state actions, because obviously this is a government-developed document after consultation with other people.

What I think is very important in the plan is that it also identifies what the key success factors are for achieving this plan. These include focused leadership, broad support of the plan across society, institutional capability, resource mobilisation and agreement on trade-offs sequencing, and willingness to prioritise and clarity of responsibility. So, in light of that, when we look at what the capacity and the will are to implement, what I would argue is that it really is about translating ideas and the plans into desired outcomes. And this we know remains a challenge for South Africa and for many countries.

In a study on implementation, Dean Fixsen, who did a review of literature on policy implementation, indicates that one of the studies he looked at says that 80 to 90 per cent of people dependent on innovations in business stop at paper implementation. So you have degrees of implementation that you can achieve. Paper implementation means that you've got the plans and policies and procedures in the place. Then you can move on to process implementation, which means that the operating procedures are in place and there are activities occurring, innovation and change language are being used but you don't see any actual changes in the functioning of the organisations or indeed in the behaviour of employees.

However, if you get to the point of a much more integrated implementation process or performance implementation, that's when you begin to see implementation producing actual results through careful and thoughtful effort at implementing the functional components of change. So when we look at the NDP we have to remember that it is a plan and it requires that we take it from the paper that it is to actual performance implementation through careful thought.

So then, still on the question of implementation, I would say that state capability remains a challenge. In addition, the private sector, its commitment and participation in effecting the NDP, in my view appears to be quite lacklustre. There needs to be mechanisms for structured engagement and building trust between business, government, labour and civil society sectors to map out an economic strategy or a social compact for the country, as has been referred to, and this is not in place. In my view, the lack of state capacity and these mechanisms undermine capacity to implement and raise questions about the will to implement the NDP.

What are the implications of South Africa's pedestrian economic performance going forward? High unemployment, especially youth unemployment, is likely to persist. South Africa is likely to miss the window of opportunity to benefit from its democratic transition. And, of course, the long-term implications of this high youth unemployment are that those who face high unemployment at the moment will have lower wages over their life cycle as well as this having a negative impact on our growth.

We will see persistent high levels of poverty and inequality because, even though we have an effective social safety net that continues to lift many people out of poverty, it's unsustainable for us to only depend on this. There needs to be higher employment and greater productivity in the economy because if we don't achieve that, even those safety nets will be threatened, let alone the goal of the NDP to increase public sector infrastructure investment to support economic growth, which will be also undermined.

So as we look forward to the next twenty years, I think the challenges will remain poverty and inequality and unemployment, particularly youth unemployment, and racial and gender inequality. And in fact, a recent study by StatsSA shows the extent of erosion of women's economic position within the society. They constitute the highest number of people who have lost jobs in a number of sectors including trade, manufacturing and agriculture. There are fewer of them that are self-employed and the barriers that they continue to face with respect to participation in the labour market remain.

I think what is also important is that if we don't deal with our spatial economy and create a more efficient and sustainable spatial economy, South Africa will continue to have significant challenges going forward. And finally, what I call fragility and resilience are going to be consistent challenges. We face policy uncertainty in a number of areas. There has to be an approach that ensures that, as different administrations come into power, they don't change so many things that the civil servants and the implementers actually feel discouraged about even implementing the new things and just wait out whoever it is that has come in at that particular point because they know the next person is going to put them through the same kinds of hoops.

Political developments globally, in my view, will also continue to pose challenges to South Africa and, because our democracy is still new, all the economic changes that we are trying to embark upon are still new. The possibility of regression always remains at the doorstep and is something that we need to guard against.

To achieve a better trajectory – some of the things have already been mentioned by Miriam – I believe that it is really urgent for us to establish a credible implementation-driven body comprised of a diverse group of South Africans that can give expression to the goals of the NDP and monitor implementation. We need to set up an almost Codesa-style process to negotiate what the priorities and trade-offs are. This is stated very clearly in the NDP and I've yet to see any sign that there is a mechanism and a process afoot to talk about what are the real trade-offs that we face and how we should prioritise our goals going forward.

We then need to mobilise state implementation agencies, business and civil society, as well as government to help to embark upon achieving those goals. We need to provide leadership development programmes for all sectors, private, public and civil society to support social cohesion and the NDP. I think if we had better leadership, in all sectors, we would probably not have had the Marikana tragedy that we experienced.

To conclude, knowledge and information sharing within and across sectors in order to reduce learning cycles and avoid reinventing the wheel are also important, particularly if you look at infrastructure and logistics. I always say that, in a country that was able to build stadia in record time and build fantastic roads for the 2010 FIFA World Cup, I just don't understand how it's possible for children to still be learning under trees, in mud huts and without any bathroom facilities. Or that, with all the fantastic logistics companies that we have, it's impossible to make sure that children have books on time and in the quantities that they require.

Job creation has already been dealt with quite at length by Miriam so I will not cover that. The final point I want to make is that we have to have a concerted effort to address black women and youth unemployment. Education and training is critical because I don't think people can access jobs, or become effective entrepreneurs, without the appropriate level of training and education. And the high transaction costs many poor and lower-income communities in our country face need to be addressed. We have access to services that people actually cannot utilise because it's simply too costly for them – whether through effort or time or money – to be able to access them. Transportation costs, dispersed settlements, lack of public transportation and various information asymmetries make it impossible for them to take advantage of all the many services that government provides.

And then finally, let's measure the impact of policy implementation and subject what is not working to review and redefine, refine or scrap it if it simply is not working to enable us to achieve our goals.

Debating Development in Post-Apartheid South Africa – Vusi Gumede

Introduction

I am going to debate 'development'. I will go through the main points quickly and then towards the end I will reflect on what I think the fundamental 'development question' is for South Africa and perhaps for Africa more broadly. It is also important to indicate, briefly, what is meant by 'development' because this input is a summary of my detailed, numerous analyses of development in post-apartheid South Africa. Development involves socio-economic progress or improvement in the well-being of people. The improvements in well-being are normally quantified through the Human Development Index (HDI), which measures human development as a composite indicator made up of life expectancy, literacy and per capita income.

Another way of thinking about development is: countries go through different stages of development, from low to higher development levels. It is generally understood that development must involve the people who need development – the people should be able to guide the development needed and also have choices for their livelihoods (as Amartya Sen[1] or Claude Ake[2] would put it). For South Africa, the debate about development has also, if not primarily, to deal with social and economic inclusion. Viewed from this perspective (i.e. social and economic inclusion), inclusive development has been slow/low in post-apartheid South Africa. Put differently, there is still a long way to go towards inclusive development in post-apartheid South Africa.

Background

I think it is useful, when we think about where South Africa is at twenty years post our political independence, to remember the many perspectives (of the national liberation movement) that have informed policies of post-apartheid South Africa. In the interest of time and space, I highlight those perspectives that I think are very instructive. Among the many perspectives, the main ones include or are captured in: the 1943 Bill of Rights in the *Africans' Claims*, the 1955 *Freedom Charter*, the 1962 *Road to South African Freedom*, the 1992 *Ready to Govern*, the 1994 *Reconstruction and Development Programme*, the 1998 *State, Property and Social Transformation* as well as the 1996 *Constitution*.

The *Ready to Govern* discussion document is probably the most important perspective compared to the others mentioned. I argue that if South Africa were able to stick to this document and its analysis, we would probably be having better social and economic outcomes today. The clarity of thought encapsulated in *Ready to Govern* implies that the society envisaged by the liberation movement could have been accomplished by now, or to a large extent, if the principles and policy propositions were followed.

However, I want to make a point that there must have been, or there is, a case to be made, perhaps, that there could have been a shift in the thinking of the liberation movement at some point during the 1940s and the mid-1950s. So when you carefully read the Bill of Rights in the *Africans' Claims* and you read the *Freedom Charter*, it seems to me that there was a shift and that we need to confront that as it has a bearing on the challenges we face today. Similarly, I want to make a related point that there might have been a departure from the *Ready to Govern* document after 1994.

From an economic point of view, there are many macroeconomic policies or political economy interventions that have been pursued since 1994 and I am not going to discuss them in the interest of time. I do mention the National Development Plan (NDP) although, really, it is not a policy document. In my view, we still do not really know what it is. It is said to be a plan; a very long document – I doubt a plan can be over 400 pages. Furthermore, its point of departure, as others have written, seems to overlook the historical experience of the various forms of enslavement of the African that the country has undergone. We seem to just want to create this new society, imagine this new society, without thinking deeply about redress and such issues. And, of course, others have written about this. Similarly, with regard to the New Growth Path (NGP), I still wonder what it is, let alone the wild targets it set: the NGP intends to increase employment by five million by 2020 and reduce narrow unemployment by 10 per cent. The NGP and its targets rely on expanding the public infrastructure programme – where would the money come from!

If you look, for instance, at the Growth, Employment and Redistribution (Gear) Framework you could argue that Gear was a macroeconomic stabilisation programme akin to a structural adjustment programme, self-imposed though. However, the Accelerated and Shared Growth Initiative for South Africa (AsgiSA), in a sense, could be argued to have been about sharing the growth, pursuing inclusive development, but from there on it is not very clear to me what these other so-called policies may be pursuing – and then, of course, a whole range of macroeconomic policies that I'm not going to go into here. I wanted to say something about a few economic and social indicators, too, but time and space do not permit.

South Africa at Twenty

South Africa has always performed badly in the economic context. It stabilised from about 1996 to about 2006, but comparatively, South Africa's economic performance has been pedestrian, relative to many comparable countries. Look at Botswana just next to South Africa, from year 2000. Look at Brazil, jump to India (I don't even include China here); go to Malaysia, which I think we could compare with because of certain similar conditions. In all these cases, if we compare our Gross Domestic Product (GDP) growth rates, they are lower compared to these countries. And the South African economy is an economy, in a sense, that has been performing below its potential.

Another issue that I thought I should talk about is comparing South Africa's level of human development with comparable countries. Again, we do very badly. If you look, for instance, from about 2000, human development in South Africa has been effectively standing still (see the United Nations Human Development Report, 2013[3]). The level of human development in South Africa has not significantly improved from about 2000. There's another way of looking at this: if you look at, for instance, the various components of human development (i.e. education, healthcare, and measure of standard of living and so on) life expectancy has declined, if you look from about 1990 to 2005. The gross national income per capita also has not really changed much if you look from 2010, in particular, to the latest data available.

Another statistic worth highlighting is the average years of schooling. The 2013 Human Development Report compares all countries' average years of schooling with expected years of schooling. In other words, a society should have a particular number of years of schooling, on average, if the whole population is taken together. And for post-apartheid South Africa, the average years of schooling have remained the same: the data implies that South Africans, on average, school five years less than expected. Since 1995, according to the 2013 Human Development Report, the expected years of schooling in South Africa are 13.1 years but the mean years of schooling have remained 8.5 years since 2010. So there is all this money we are pumping into education but there is no change – we are not catching up with the expected years of schooling, let alone the quality of schooling.

And then there is an issue of income inequality. When looking at the Gini coefficient, a commonly used measure of income inequality, either from the expenditure side or from the income side, the trend is similar. Contrary to what many people say, it is not true that income inequality in the African population group has been the main driver of income inequality in post-apartheid South Africa. In fact, the people that are driving high income inequality in South Africa are the white population group. This makes sense because of their economic status: they are already well-off due to their investments that ensure whites become better off over time, while we also know that many Africans are not getting jobs. So, many Africans are unemployed relative to whites, of course, relative to Indians and Coloureds – and Africans bear the brunt of hardship disproportionately to other population groups in South Africa. It should be acknowledged, though, that the income inequality within the African population group had increased in the 1990s to mid-2000s as some Africans were getting well-paying jobs while many Africans were remaining unemployed. However, from the mid- to late-2000s, income inequality within the African population group has remained effectively unchanged while that of the whites has increased. I have elaborated this view elsewhere.[4]

South Africa's Development Challenge

Many people have argued that part of the challenge South Africa faces has to do with the transition: our transition from apartheid to post-apartheid society or to a democratic society – Patrick Bond, Hein Marais and Sampie Terreblanche talk of the *elite transition*. The people who have written about South Africa's political transition – you may disagree with them – make their case well, which simply argues that the post-apartheid development experience has to be understood within the context of our transition from apartheid to a post-apartheid society or to a democratic society. In other words, many compromises were made that do not allow society to move forward faster.

Roger Southall,[5] for instance, has characterised South Africa's transition as a 'reform bargain', drawing from Scott Taylor's 'reform coalition'. Southall (2010, p. 5) explains the reform bargain as a 'mechanism that facilitated South Africa's success which was underpinned by the new government's commitment to providing the opportunities for large-scale business to internationalise'. Again, a particular compromise was reached. And on the more radical side, John Saul[6] argues that nothing much has really changed in South Africa because the economy is still subject to the control, manipulation and so forth of the global capitalist system.

There are some scholars – see for instance recent books by Adam Habib[7] and Gillian Hart[8] – who have been trying to deal with similar issues from a different point of view and I thought I would highlight what they conclude: that South Africa needs a new political settlement, something along the lines of a social pact; something along the lines of a social contract. I argue that I do not think that it is feasible yet to do that. So we may need to go back to the drawing board.

More broadly, in the context of the continent as a whole, many scholars have looked at the transformation of the continent and make a point that the challenge that the developing world and Africa, in particular, face, has to do with the 'development merchant system' – Adebayo Adedeji,[9] in a powerful speech he gave in a conference in 2002, argued that 'the implementation of an exogenous agenda has, perforce, been pursued because of the operation of the development merchant system under which foreign-crafted economic reform policies have been turned into a new kind of special goods which are largely and quickly financed by the operators of the development merchant system, regardless of the negative impact such policies have on the African economies and polities' (p. 4).

Taking what Adedeji says, and what other like-minded scholars say, the development merchant system ensures a deliberate design by the global capitalist order to perpetuate a socio-economic and political system that advances the interests of the West and maintains the peripheralisation of the African continent. Our colleagues – take, for instance, Sabelo Ndlovu-Gatsheni – characterise the development merchant system, broadly or differently, as an aspect of the 'colonial matrix of power'. In his 2012 Inaugural Professorial Lecture, Ndlovu-Gatsheni[10] argued that 'African political economies have remained hostage to invisible colonial matrices of power' (p. 3). So it is not by chance that the African continent remains at the bottom, and every time it comes up with a programme, an alternative development programme (such as the Lagos Plan of Action, the Abuja Treaty, the African Alternative Framework to Structural Adjustment Programme for Socio-Economic Recovery and Transformation, the New Partnership for Africa's Development, etc.) there is some interference that slows down progress – many others have made this or similar points.[11] And I think we need to think about it from a theoretical perspective: whether this also applies in our context in South Africa.

Concluding Remarks

The main point that this input makes is that countries, at a minimum, need appropriate policies and should sequence reforms accordingly. It could be argued that South Africa has done relatively well in some instances of policymaking: Gear, for instance, was a macroeconomic stabilisation intervention in which the immediate and obtaining context at the time was perhaps dictated by the post-Cold War dispensation. I am not discussing the merits, or lack thereof, of Gear. I am simply saying that it could be argued that Gear was attending to a pertinent context at the time. Once the economy was stabilised, a different economic policy should have been pursued. Before AsgiSA, arguably, there was a gap in economic policy. After AsgiSA, I argue, there has not been a comprehensive economic policy. As indicated earlier, the NGP and the NDP are not policies. Perhaps these are broad political-economy interventions. One area that comes closer to being an economic policy is the Industrial Policy Action Plan, but it is mainly about the industrialisation of the South African economy, not a comprehensive policy for the economy as a whole.

I take it for granted that it is generally agreed that implementation is critical. With regards to policy, I argue that the hard choices that need, or needed, to be made have not been made. This input also makes a point – a theoretical issue that still needs further elaboration – that the post-apartheid South African economy appears to be a compromise between the African majority and the white minority who hold greater economic power. South Africa's political economy after 1994 appears to have been defined by a paradox of growth, stagnation and recession.

Another point I have been arguing for some time now is: we need to reconfigure state-capital relations. It seems to me that the socio-economic challenges in South Africa start around 2006/2007 and this, I argue, had a lot to do with the lack of policy reforms. To be sure, I was still in government at that time – I left government in 2009. Therefore, policy challenges are not new, but what seems to be happening is that the state is increasingly getting captured by capital: what government is pursuing, largely, is shaped by the interests of the private sector. We do need to address or reconfigure those state-capital relations. The last point is that a new vision for South Africa's political economy is overdue: the NDP could have been about a new vision for the economy rather than the long list of issues, priorities and debatable targets. The historical experience of apartheid colonialism and its ramifications should be informing policies that post-apartheid South Africa pursues, particularly twenty years since political independence, in order that South Africa could ultimately become the 'nation' that many sacrificed lives for.

End Notes

1. Sen, A. 1999. *Development as Freedom*. New York: Anchor.
2. Ake, C. 2000. *Democracy and Development in Africa*. Maryland: Brookings Institution.
3. United Nations Development Programme. 2013. *Human Development Report* 2013. New York: Palgrave Macmillan.
4. See, for instance, Gumede. 2015. 'Inequality in Post-apartheid South Africa.' In Mangcu, X. (ed.), *The Colour of Our Future*. Johannesburg: Wits University Press.
5. Southhall, R. 2010. 'South Africa 2010: From Short-term Success to Long-term Decline?' in Daniel, J., Naidoo, P., Pillay, D. and Southall, R. (2010) (eds.), *New South African Review* 1: 2010: 'Development or Decline?' Johannesburg: Wits University Press.
6. Saul, J. 2012. 'Globalisation, Recolonisation and the Paradox of Liberation in Southern Africa' in Lissoni, A., Soske, J., Erlank, N., Nieftagodien, N. and Bashda, O. (2012) (eds.), *One Hundred Years of the ANC: Debating Liberation Histories Today*. Johannesburg: Wits University Press.
7. Habib, A. 2013. *South Africa's Suspended Revolution: Hopes & Prospects*. Johannesburg: Wits University Press.
8. Hart, G. 2013. *Rethinking the South African Crisis: Nationalism, Populism and Hegemony*. Scottsville: UKZN Press.
9. Adedeji, A. 2002. 'From the Lagos Plan of Action to the New Partnership for Africa's Development and from the Final Act of Lagos to the Constitutive Act: Wither Africa?' Keynote address to the African Forum for Envisioning Africa, Nairobi, Kenya, 26–29 April.
10. Ndlovu-Gatsheni, S. 2012. 'Coloniality of Power in Development Studies and the Impact of Global Imperial Designs on Africa'. Inaugural Professorial Lecture, 16 October 2012, University of South Africa.
11. See, for instance, Mkandawire, T. 2011. 'Running While Others Walk: Knowledge and the Challenge of Africa's Development'. *Africa Development*, Vol. xxxvi. No. 2, pp. 1–36.

PART 3

VALUES, NATION FORMATION AND SOCIAL COMPACTING

Values matter in the provision of foundations for political stability and economic growth. Democratic South Africa needs to develop mechanisms for securing sufficient consensus from all stakeholders – in civil society, government, industry – to put shoulders to the wheel behind its founding constitutional blueprint and the NDP Vision 2030. Arguably, how this should be achieved beyond institutional platforms like the National Economic Development and Labour Council (Nedlac) will require the active engagement of social institutions such as unions, schools, family, religious bodies, business councils and professional associations. The question, though, is: how to ensure the attainment of socio-economic rights for all South Africans, transcend the phase of political compacting and unite the nation beyond occasional high-profile events? Can South Africans empathise with 'the other' (defined, for instance, by social status, language and race)? Can they develop a common view of present challenges and unite in efforts geared towards providing 'a better life for all'? Can the collective spirit that galvanised the struggle against apartheid and the political settlement be reignited towards active democratic citizenship? What contributions and sacrifices should be expected of the various social actors?

Values, Nation formation and Social Compacting –
Trevor Manuel

Good afternoon. I think the task is a pretty complex one – 'values, nation building and social compacts' – and I want to start from the position perhaps where Justice Moseneke was this morning; something that Dr Ginwala touched on as well. If we look at values in society then I think we must go back to the foundational document, which is our constitution. The preamble and the founding provisions set out the task; the values of citizenship are set out in the founding provisions and the preamble commits us, for instance, to raising the living standards of all citizens and freeing the potential of each person. It's not a once-off, it's continuous, and so I think that part of what the discussion invites is a question as to whether we go back and revisit those values in our constitution because they are meant to be durable.

In many respects, I think that, for me, the starting point about our constitution is in fact the grand compact as well. That's what it is. That's what its origin is, and I think we must discuss the Constitution in the context of origin. The key challenge for us as we go back, and I think it impacts on the way we construct the nation as well, is whether we have a government that is continually trusted, and there are two criteria that I think would be important in this regard.

The first is that you must have functional institutions. All the institutions, and our constitution creates a myriad of them, must be functional, deemed to be competent and deemed to be able to respond to what is required of them. The second issue that is fundamental is that leadership must be deemed to be competent. And one of the points that one makes in the context of compacts generally, is that they work if you have an external force capable of convening contending forces so that you can arrive, not just at solutions, but focus on implementation as you go forward.

In many ways, the starting point for us is a difficult one because, in the context of nation building, we start off from an appreciation of just how complex South Africans, all of us who occupy this same geographic space, are. We speak eleven different languages. There are many class variations. We come from different histories. Part of what apartheid did was actually to emphasise what divided us. And so, reconstructing this into a single nation, I think, is always going to be exceedingly important: a challenge, and we must understand the challenge and develop matrices so that we can deal with issues. Part of what we will have within that history is the inequality of assets, incomes, education and work opportunities, and these things don't disappear by fiat, you've got to work at them, and the way in which you construct compacts therefore must help us work through these issues on a continuing basis.

Now when we turn to the issue of compacts, I want to share a thought from Professor Mkandawire. He says social compacts are not self-sustaining equilibria. They often need an external actor to provide the framework for negotiations and for ensuring respect by all parties for the conditions of the bargain. The predispositions of the state towards various actors can facilitate social pacts. The state can help by providing a credible societal vision and coordinating the expectations of different social constituencies.

My submission to you is that, in many ways, the Constitution at the start of this process (it's only eighteen-and-a-half years old, May 1996) provides that societal vision. It sets it out in the Preamble and it affirms what we seek in the Founding Provisions. And then you can take through the Bill of Rights and whatever follows. And you know, later, much later (because there's division), we try and reconvene this through a societal vision in the context of the National Development Plan. But in and of itself it doesn't produce the change. The compact, to be effective, must be worked at, and I think that Mkandawire speaks to that external force capable of convening.

Now one of the challenges is that sometimes we convene people to talk, and we talk, and we reach a point, and we develop a communiqué, and then we walk away because there aren't any measurements for implementation. So my sense is that – whether you are talking about the Jobs Summit, the Growth Summit, the Youth Accord, or more recently, and still very fresh in our minds, the Labour Market Accord of just last week – unless we have instruments in place that can measure and be accountable for these things, the accords actually come to nought. And that's a fear because I think that, in the absence, cynicism sets in.

So I want to end, so that we can have more time for discussion, by saying that even our constitution is a document that we must view in a very dynamic context. If all that we have is ownership of this great document, our constitution – if we only own it as a nation it would come to nought. We have to live and relive; we have to energise and re-energise. We have to take stock of the deviation from the intent of that negotiation that produced a document in May of 1996. And be committed, and I think again, Justice Moseneke, you helped us lift out some of those issues in your presentation this morning about what experience has now taught us and how we take it forward, mindful of the fact that we don't want to unravel the entire knitting that went into it. But we must be prepared in an honest and open way to recommit to re-energising our constitution.

Values, Nation formation and Social Compacting – **Albie Sachs**

I am going to tell a little story about my first contact with our co-host, Joel Netshitenzhe. It's a very trivial story, and my fear is you will remember that trivial story about a trivial activity long after you have remembered the more serious things that I'm going to say. Quite some years ago, on an anniversary of the launch of the armed struggle, Joel, in his capacity as editor of *Mayibuye*, the ANC publication, asked for people to contribute stories about their participation in the armed struggle. And I'm sitting at my desk working and I say to myself: I am going to offer the most trivial participation of anyone in the armed struggle. And it took place in 1961, in fact before the launch of the armed struggle. I'm sitting in my chambers as an advocate in Cape Town. There's a knock on the door. Somebody comes in and he bends down. He takes a little piece of paper out of his sock. He holds it up, gives it to me, and tells me that in half an hour somebody else is going to come in for that piece of paper. So I put that piece of paper in my sock and wait. Sure enough, after half an hour, there's a knock on the door and somebody comes in. I take the piece of paper out of my sock, I give it to him, he puts it in his sock and he goes out. That, I later discovered, was the sum total of my role in the armed struggle. Sometime later, something that somebody said made me realise that the little piece of paper might have contained the Umkhonto we Sizwe oath. And so, by keeping the oath in my sock for thirty minutes, I made my contribution to the armed struggle. I sent this story off to Joel thinking it would merely raise a smile. But it was published! And in fact I was very impressed because I thought it was important to have a sense of humour and understanding of the diversity of the participations in what was so often simply reduced to abstract incantations about 'our glorious people's army' and a 'glorious people's struggle'.

In any event, thinking about values, I began to think of a butterfly. It's a beautiful creature that flutters with lovely colours. You take that creature and you capture it and you pin it on a board and put it in a box. Is it still a butterfly? It's got the wings. It's got the colours. But it's not fluttering: there's no motion, no beauty. And values are like that. If you over-define value you are somehow taking the value out of value. It's got to have an element of poetry, of longing, of dreams, of selflessness, if you like. And yet, it cannot only be poetic in a way that makes it free-floating and ineffective. So the presentation I am going to make now is about poetry and science, science and poetry. These, to my mind, are the foundation of values.

I thought back about what had been the big moments in the last twenty years when the theme of South Africans coming together, overcoming all the barriers, doing something jointly, had been most intensely meaningful. Four very disparate moments just popped into my head.

The first, of course, was the election itself. It was quite remarkable and people still cry when they remember that day when we stood in line, so many of us. So it was the action of voting together in one election that was defeating all the notions of the impossibility of South Africans living together in one country. It was hugely exemplary and educative. We didn't have somebody going around and patting us on the back and saying, congratulations, you are doing a marvellous thing compacting the nation in this way. Rather, the education came through the sheer extensiveness of the participation, the almost randomness of where you found yourself in the line, and the fact that we could do it at all.

The second moment that comes to mind, not quite as complete: sport, the rugby world cup. I know one of my co-panellists had big doubts about its significance. But South Africans love a party, and this was just a chance to somehow celebrate and be joyful about something. And it was very unexpected. The victory was unexpected and the jubilation was unexpected.

The third (I mightn't get the sequence right), it just popped into my head: 'I am an African' – the solemnly-delivered speech in Parliament by Thabo Mbeki. Though I may often have criticised Thabo about other things, I will never, never forget that moment. And what was it about? It wasn't just the poetry of the language. It was the styling, the presence, the fact that, in this august body that's normally rather formal where people get at each other with petty points, something poured out that just expressed the longings and hopes of so many people in a very embracing and very, very inclusive way.

Perhaps the most prolonged period of that sense of South Africaness in all its excellence and fun and tribulation, of course, was the Soccer World Cup. And of course the Soccer World Cup, for those of us who remember how extraordinary it was – the feeling, even though our team didn't do well – wasn't just about success. It was the success of accomplishing the World Cup: of organising it, the joy of people participating and watching and arguing and debating. It was like ten days to a couple of weeks of a nation on holiday.

I bring this out not simply as little moments of nostalgia, but to illustrate what I believe is a stronger point. This social compacting is not something that you bring about through a National Development Plan. The Plan could well have the result of creating social compacting. But you don't put social compacting as such in a plan. You create the conditions for it to emerge through a plan. I still remember when I was in Mozambique at a meeting with a guy from the GDR, the German Democratic Republic, responsible for culture. There were hardly any people there. I felt he'd come a long way and they were giving us a lot of support. I wanted to offer some delicate hint about culture in the GDR. So I said, from a cultural point of view, that there was tremendous support for theatre, such as the Berliner Ensemble of Berthold Brecht. But wasn't there a lack of lightness, of humour, of variety? And he confidently answered: 'Don't worry, comrade, we have a plan for culture, and it provides that in the coming year we are going to train four comedians.'

And what I am going to urge today is that we avoid that kind of approach: that we don't think we can produce a genuine and deep sense of all being South Africans by simply running up the flag and getting everybody to salute it. Maybe we should regularly salute the flag, maybe not. But that's not the way real cohesion between South Africans will be brought about. It's when we are doing things jointly that we all believe in – things that are credible – that we come together. We come into the new evolving consciousness not because we are obeying some kind of command to the effect that thou shall be compacted and thou shall love thy neighbour! The shared consciousness emerges because we believe there's a credibility to the very actions that we are doing. Sometimes, with the best intentions but uneven methodology, we end up with inadequate results. I was thinking of the different sites of memory of the apartheid era. Driving up here last night, I saw the beautiful lights up on the hill. I just wonder how many people in this room have been to Freedom Park. Can you indicate? I see it's quite a large number. How many go regularly to Freedom Park? Now it's a very small number. It's a magnificent site. It's beautifully conceived and developed. Yet it's not working. It can work. It will work. I believe it will work. The framework is there. But now it's not working. We should ask what is the missing ingredient. There are lovely constructions in that extraordinary place with great symbolical meaning. What is lacking?

Part of the answer may come from Freedom Square. This big monumental place built on the site of Kliptown where the Freedom Charter was adopted, is deserted. It's actually sad to see. The only energy there comes from the people selling oranges and knitting and so on under these enormous arches. Occasionally, commemorative meetings are held there – it's invoked. The idea was to bring about a sense of development and national memory and so on and it's not working. It seems too forced, too imposed, a representation of an idea. The empty monumentality severs us rather than connects us with the past. As one of those who was there when the police surrounded us at the Congress of the People, I feel saddened rather than elated when I go there. We must learn from what is lacking. I'm sure Freedom Square will still have its day.

The Constitutional Court, to my mind, and I'm not just saying this out of personal pride having been a judge there, it does work. A court built in the heart of the Old Fort Prison where Gandhi and Mandela were locked up works, because there is something intense and real and meaningful about it today. It works because it's functioning. It's not just a monument. It's a living place. And then the other institutions connected with the defence of the Constitution: the Commission for Gender Equality sitting over the Women's Jail, and these things are working and functioning. Some would like to see them working better than they do, but somehow that's a form of memory and a site of memory that brings people together, reminds us of the past and uses the past in a way that helps us to develop the future. That's what is lacking at Freedom Square, and begging to be invoked in Freedom Park. Solemn incantations of the past imposed on the present actually become alienating and undermine inclusion and social cohesion. They lack true vitality and community involvement. They seek dutiful obedience rather than genuine empowering respect.

I would like to conclude (or begin my conclusion rather than promise an immediate conclusion) by picking up on what Dikgang Moseneke said this morning. I was asked on the way down here: 'Comrade Albie, how do you feel about all these things happening in the country? Do you feel this is what you were fighting for?' And I say, when I look at this country, yes, this is the country that I was fighting for, but many things that are happening here are not at all what I was fighting for. Lots of things are awful and impermissible and indefensible. One of the saddest things to see these days is people defending the indefensible, rather than saying how can we overcome the indefensible? You are in a hole, you dig in your heels, you dig deeper and deeper and you get deeper and deeper into the hole and you don't get out of it. But for all the shocks and setbacks, we've not got what happened in Mozambique where I lived for eleven years after independence: huge transformation followed by a terrible civil war: millions of refugees; thousands of limbs lost to landmines. I was in Tahrir Square in Egypt after Mubarak fell; the jubilation in the streets was wonderful. Now the Prime Minister is in jail; the army took over. We have a functioning country. We have elections every five years. The President steps down. We have a strong independent judiciary. I feel so proud of having been part of that judiciary and to see the judgments that are coming out today and to see the way in which people from all sectors of our society feel, if we have a problem (and I agree we shouldn't send all our problems to the judiciary), there is one institution at least that people feel we don't have to go out in the streets and try and kill each other to get our point of view across. We can take the matter to court.

I think it's a huge achievement, in the world, not just in South Africa. And there is something about the style, the manner in which we on the Court worked: how we should be addressed, so that we shouldn't be called 'My Lord'. The fact that we are seated at the level of counsel, we are not seated high up there. Lots of little details went into making this an acceptable South African institution. The very building itself. We have created a new paradigm for the world. We haven't copied an English courthouse or the American Supreme Court. We have built our own type of court that is rooted in our culture, in our society, that people feel comfortable with and welcomed when they go there.

The place, the process, the style of work, the openness, the seriousness, the warmth and the direct and ongoing connection with the Constitution all ensure the continuing evolution of new South African values in a most productive and meaningful way. Yes, the Court does settle disputes. But most importantly, it also deals with deep issues of public morality, with what it means to be a South African today. And the very composition of the Constitutional Court, the way it works, promotes the values of unity in diversity. The one part of South Africa, to be quite candid, where I don't feel I am white, is when I go up to the Constitutional Court. It's a little liberated zone that has its own cultural resonance: a space where I don't feel I am a white person in a white area, or a white person in a Black area. And for me, in that sense, the very building, the style of work, and the way it addresses people – all these different features provide a living practical example of the themes that were presented in the title of this section.

Now to conclude my conclusion, the German political philosopher, Habermas, round about the late 1980s, dealt with an issue that had cropped up very powerfully in his country. Lots of people were saying we Germans must dig deep into our traditions and our culture and the history of Germany to create a shared patriotism so that everybody who is German could feel proud to be German. Habermas rejected that approach. He said what we need is constitutional patriotism. What makes us proud to be Germans is that we reconstructed our country after the defeat of Naziism; that we found ways of expressing in the German language the values of constitutional patriotism, which draw deeply from our culture and history, but emphasise, above all, the pride that comes from the fact that we have dialogue, that we have debate, that we have diversity, that we recognise freedom of expression, that we regard each other as equals, respect the dignity of all and take joy from the multiplicity of voices in the country.

And that's what I feel gives me great pride in being a South African – the fact that we have a diversity, we acknowledge it, we don't try and suppress it to make everybody stand to attention and salute in a particular way. We have a lot of humour. We recognise the importance of dialogue. Dialogue, dialogue, dialogue. We got our constitution out of dialogue. I don't like the word compromise. I like the word accommodation. Accommodation is principled. Accommodation recognises there are other people there with their views, their positions and their longings. How can we live together? How can we find a common foundation rather than looking at the other and saying: if you do a deal with me, I'll do a deal with you, we'll give each other a little bit. It's not that at all. It's a deep, principled way in a very diverse society of finding the means of living together.

So, the three Ds then would be my answer: dignity, dialogue and difference. In addition to the points that have been referred to by the chairperson earlier on, the Constitution itself is a value-laden document. It's not just a technical document about structures of government. It's about the value of being a citizen, of being a human being, being a South African, being a man, being a woman, being gay, being straight, being Zulu-speaking, being Tswana-speaking, being English-speaking, being whatever you are. All of that is recognised in our constitution. Affirmatively, positively, rather than trying to reconfigure and re-jig our constitution, we've got to see and realise its full promise. We've got to find ways and means of living out everything that the Constitution promises. In that way, I believe, we will gradually, step by step, achieve the themes that are in the title of this presentation. Come to think of it, I've even forgotten the actual words of the title. But I know they are very nice and whatever they are, we must aim to live up to them.

VALUES, NATION FORMATION AND SOCIAL COMPACTING –
PREGS GOVENDER

Thanks very much. It's hard to be at the tail-end of a very, very long day. I'd like to begin with Pat McFadden's question about whether we need a bloodless revolution. And how do we turn to the roots of what the problems are, and how do we address those roots? I work for the South African Human Rights Commission and, for the last few years, I've been working on the rights to water and sanitation. And what we have seen is what we all know: that rights are indivisible; that human beings, like our rights, can't be fragmented; that rights are interdependent, they are interrelated.

So what our work on water and sanitation has shown is how deeply entrenched the apartheid spatial geography remains in our country twenty years into our democracy. And a key part of that is the reality that the majority of those who are poorest, who have lost their jobs in the last few years as StatsSA's figures show, the majority of those who are now in precarious employment in the so-called informal sector, in casualised labour, are women and young girls. Those who spend the most time collecting water, looking for clean water, despite the fact that there was a commitment to free basic services, a CoGTA study showed that over 80 per cent of the people in the municipalities that they surveyed were not registered as indigent to be able to access those free services.

What we also saw, and this is a critical question, is that 95 per cent of rural water in our country is used by 1.2 per cent, and that 1.2 per cent is mainly white agribusiness, mining and the tourist industry. So absolutely, we have to address the issues of efficiencies, corruption, etc. But we have to address the question of equality and ownership of resources and in whose interest policy is made and implemented. Because the heart of the values enshrined in our constitution – of dignity, equality, social justice, non-racism, non-sexism, open responsive government, accountable government – at the heart of that is how we value people, and who is valued, and what is valued, and whose work is valued.

All of the studies have shown that, to address the right to food, for example, we have to address the role of women, across our continent, not just in our country, as subsistence farmers, as small farmers. The recently launched Oxfam report on hunger in our country begins with the story of Nthabiseng, born in a rural village. Based on current statistics, Oxfam estimates that Nthabiseng is almost one-and-a-half times as likely to die in the first year of her life. She will be lucky if she gets one year of schooling. Such basics as clean toilets, clean water or decent health care will be out of her reach. If Nthabiseng has children there is a very high chance that they will also grow up equally poor.

In Limpopo, which is income-poor, where there are very few paying jobs, the UN Special Rapporteur on his visit to our country a few years ago found that there were actually much higher levels of food security than anticipated. And the reason for that was because of women's unpaid contribution: unrecognised, unvalued contribution in terms of subsistence farming. Subsistence farming is not counted as a contribution to the GDP, unless things have changed. Yet the submarines that we bought that sit in Cape Town's harbour, the purchase of those did contribute to our GDP. In a global war economy, armaments increase the GDP. The fallouts from war, the need to build hospitals to treat people, etc. count as contributions to GDP. But the work of sustaining people across our continent is not counted as a contribution to the GDP.

I listened quite intently to some of the presentations earlier on, and I was thinking about who it is who's contributing to growth and what's counted as growth and why it is important to problematise growth. And I was thinking about the fact that India's new leader oversaw the Gujarat massacre: but he also ensured foreign direct investment in Gujarat that increased growth in Gujarat, which was one of the key reasons for his support by the private sector across the world that ensured his rise to power.

So the question of who it is that we looked to when we were trying to forge a society that honours the values in our constitution, what is it that we need to be addressing in terms of who holds power and in whose interests critical decisions are made? In South Africa, and I think in many parts of the world, when you think of the wastage of water the image that is used is a dripping tap in a poor community. How many of you have seen that? A dripping tap in a poor community, in our news reports, etc. Yet, the biggest waster of water is industry. The biggest polluter of water is industry. Yet, recently in parliament, the Minister and her department clarified that over 40 mining companies are operating without water licences.

So the question is, in the context of the fact that 67 per cent of African children live below the poverty line, if we don't fundamentally, radically, have that bloodless revolution, who is it that we serve when we make key policy choices? In terms of food, most of our seed is now owned by global corporations such as Monsanto. You know that that seed can't be used the way seed traditionally is reused, because that seed is terminator seed. We are one of the few countries, if not the only country in the world, which has allowed our staple food to be genetically modified.

So when we look at values and when we look at social compacting, we have to be able to look at in whose interests and who is it that we are valuing. We know that there is significant tax evasion in our country by huge corporations and wealthy individuals. And I think the figure runs into tens of millions. I'm sure, Trevor Manuel, with your past hat, you could clarify exactly how many billions that constitutes. Who pays for water (and I'm using water as the example to illustrate something that applies to many other areas, many other rights)? Who pays for water? And the fact that, even recently, CoGTA talked about one of the most critical problems being the non-payment for services, and we are talking about services in poor communities across our country; they are not talking about the fact that those who use most of South Africa's water is industry.

Earlier this year, four people were killed in a water protest in Madibeng. Madibeng means place of water. The Madibeng municipality is the area in which Marikana is situated. When we went to investigate the talk that you'd heard was between a woman leader from Marikana and me, what they showed us was that, when you enter Marikana, the electricity pylons that you will see on your left-hand side next to the mines ensure electricity to the mines. And the woman said to us that often they have no electricity. They have no electricity and that water in many parts of their areas often comes on only at night. So they have to go and collect water at night in the dark.

Now if you are going to address gender-based violence in our country, or across our world, we can't do it without looking at what are the policy decisions that devalue women's lives, that make women vulnerable and make girls vulnerable to gender-based violence, to the brutalisation of poverty and inequality, to the fact that they are the ones taking care of children, of people with illnesses including HIV and AIDS. In a way, where even our budget recently in the Free State, dismissed huge numbers of community care workers who are doing that work with a stipend, with a tiny stipend. So the issue of values is to understand, to recognise the work, the huge amount of work that people are doing every day, and to recognise the stigma that existed during apartheid where people who were Black, poor, female, were deeply stigmatised as being lazy, as being ... come on, you can remember all the stereotypes. I'm sure you can. Every single one of us can.

So why, twenty years into our democracy, do those stereotypes continue to permeate policy choices? Well, we do not recognise the contribution; we do not ensure that people have the resources necessary. I want to end with a quote from the Universal Declaration of Human Rights, and I think it's about section 27 of the Declaration; it is quite far down, right at the end. It says that, to be able to realise the rights in the Universal Declaration, you have to have a social and international order in which rights can be realised. The social and international order that we have right now is one in which women's work is what is creating our laptops, our computers, our cellphones, very, very cheaply, at the cost that we have spoken about: the costs are very, very high. So the push for the cheapest labour across the country, across the world and in our country, has seen the loss of jobs in the formal economy and has seen an increasing casualisation of work, work that is precarious, and it is women and girls who are doing that work in the main. And unless we factor that into our policy choices, the values in our Constitution are just words on paper, and we can't afford to let that happen.

Beyond Social Compacting: A Power Matrix in Flux in Post-Mandela South Africa – Mazibuko Jara

I've entitled this talk 'Going Beyond Social Compacting' and a subtitle suggesting that perhaps there's a power matrix that's in flux, perhaps in stresses and strains in a post-apartheid, or rather post-Mandela South Africa. I hope it becomes apparent as to why I chose this. So that what that means is that I may fall short of some of the questions that were posed as a challenge to this panel. In summary, what I'm putting forward is fairly controversial. Firstly, I'm quite convinced that, if we are to have a social compact or a process of social compacting of genuine substantive dialogue and agreement, then we have to realise that our ruling elite is incapable of overcoming its own limits. What it has done over the last twenty years is to manage basically a legitimate popular process of political democratisation, but it left the structural and systemic foundations of our economy intact. A lot has been said in that regard already.

Despite the NDP, I'm quite convinced that the ruling elite is strategically incapable of mobilising all of us behind a national vision of transformation that goes to the heart of the problems that face this society. As part of its limitations, we're seeing it being increasingly intolerant of dissent, of different perspectives and even different social forces. In fact, when it comes to tribal governance, we're actually seeing very sustained efforts to deliberately entrench systems of social control that actually go against some of the values in the Constitution. That's enough for the political elite as a critique for now.

In addition to the political elite, what you then have is a ruling class that has not been able to meet its part of the bargain: not just unable, but also quite unwilling. Instead, legitimately perhaps, it has benefited immensely from the changes we have seen. The shame of apartheid is gone. Sasol can now be a multinational company and then what was required, in terms of the compromise of 1994, was for Sasol or other South African capital to play particular roles, and we're not seeing that ruling class playing that part.

When it comes to the people, despite faith in the ANC without a doubt, South Africa is a society of a disillusioned people, who have not, as Justice Moseneke was saying, tested how far the Constitution goes: how far can people claim that constitution. Even though there's massive ANC hegemony amongst the mass of the people, it's interesting and important to note that there is a small but critical minority who are starting to take some conscious first steps towards challenging ANC hegemony. Now, whilst this is still maturing, as a person who studies these questions and perhaps is active amongst these emerging social forces, I think what we're seeing are the beginnings of some profound underlying shifts that could have destabilising effects for any notion of a social compact or even the political legitimacy of the ruling elite.

Does this suggest, then, a deep rupture with the consensus we have had since the early 1990s? I think there are strong suggestions in that direction. The decline of ANC voter support in the major metros (except for in KwaZulu-Natal), whether it's Gauteng, whether it's Port Elizabeth, whether it's Cape Town, that for me sends a fairly strong signal about how there are the beginnings of people expressing some deep rupture. And, of course, then Marikana, the various sustained social explosions: 11,000 of them in the last year, and what is happening now in the trade union movement. I read these as not just unhappiness over service delivery or over e-tolls, but actually some indirect unexpressed questioning of the economic dimensions of the post-1994 social consensus.

I don't think people are revolting against the political framework of democracy, of equality of rights as in the Constitution, but there are fundamental questions being asked about the economy, in particular. If there are possibilities or suggestions of this deep rupture, what then does it mean for renewed efforts at a social compact going forward with the NDP as a foundation? What does it mean for the legitimacy and effectiveness of the ANC as the main political guarantor of stability? Presumably, a social compact, or the process of a social compact, will require that kind of a role-player in addition to what Trevor Manuel was saying in relation to an external force, bringing the contending forces together. I think there are some serious questions being asked by society about the capacity of the ANC as a guarantor of such a process.

Now I'm going into some detail, putting forward what I think are some constraints to dialogue, some constraints to social compacting. The fact that our townships, our informal settlements, our inner cities, our rural villages, are zones of rotting means that the most important social force in this society is not able to be a game player in a process of dialogue. The working class is turning on itself in big ways. Solidarity is breaking down. Against the values of the Constitution, we're seeing a rise in social conservatism in ways that could possibly delegitimise some of the values that we celebrate in the Constitution. Instead of the kind of deliberate democratic or generative discussions that you saw up till the mid-1990s, there's weakening in a significant way of self-organisation. No matter what one thinks politically of what is happening in Cosatu, but the decay of Cosatu and what is likely to be a very painful restructuring of the labour movement, are also going to add to the absence of an effective social force as a contributor to the process of social dialogue.

A further constraint that we're likely to see in the coming period is the obvious question about succession in the ANC and in government. As the Nkandla debacle has shown us, there's quite a serious erosion of public faith in the political elite and the capacity of state institutions. It's not just the Nkandla debacle. In my work in Keiskammahoek, we have tried for the last twelve years to say to the Department of Education that we can mobilise volunteer teachers, volunteer students and we have secured money for this so that we can actually just improve Grade 12 passes. We can't get a single meeting. We can't get a single principal to commit to a series of steps that they must undertake. That's just one small example of how state institutions are just not able to function as institutions that are required to play a role such that in many parts, I think elsewhere in the country too, but at least in many parts of the Eastern Cape, people have no faith whatsoever once you talk about bringing government into the process as a role-player. At best, what people seek to do is to secure the most resources as quickly as possible from a government department, but otherwise keep government far and out from the process of development. And that is a major crisis. I'm not celebrating it. The state should be playing a very decisive and active role in very many dimensions of our lives.

Now, Adam Habib talks about the experience of South-East Asian countries as having been driven by a coalition of reformers within and outside the state and my conclusion, thinking about Habib's point, is that we do not have a critical mass of reformers within the state who can then smartly and effectively work with forces outside the state to drive a common vision. Despite what the NDP hopes for, the delegitimisation of the 1996 constitution by the political elite is also a major problem because it is opening the door to conservative forces to delegitimise it but also, on the other hand, the ANC finds it almost impossible to claim and defend its own constitution and is thus opening another door to forces on the right to claim that constitution. So, for me, I think, Comrade Trevor, what you are raising, I agree with in regard to how we need to reclaim the constitution from below, but the major barrier to that is this conscious effort, whether it's Blade Ndzimande's references to anti-majoritarianism or liberal forces and so on, in ways that then make it possible for people to connect with that constitution in a way that they can use it. All of these problems – constraints I'm pointing to – then mean that there's huge space for capital to have a free hand to do all sorts of things without being effectively engaged; without feeling uncomfortable; without feeling awkward in ways that it should because of the role the state is playing, but also because of the lack of effective organisation of workers and poor people outside of the state.

If you look at a map of traditional councils in terms of the Traditional Leadership and Governance Framework Act of 2003, that's basically spaces of tribal governance, reproducing almost, as it were, the apartheid homeland maps. Not surprisingly, that same geographical space is also the space of the highest levels of poverty. If you were to engage with the rural development chapter of the NDP, you're talking about people who are in poverty and are increasingly subject to undemocratic rule, which is problematic in many ways, against the values of the Constitution and, therefore, almost displaced as social actors who can engage in this social space in social dialogue.

Now here is my major point of controversy: I don't think there's a problem with the notion of a National Development Plan, but if you're sitting within what I consider the limited prism of the National Planning Commission, then indeed there has been substantial consultation; then indeed the National Development Plan is widely endorsed by society. But if you look at that rural development chapter again, take the Amathole District where I'm located, various research reports suggest that it has 25 per cent of small farmers in the country. I work with a number of groups, including a group calling itself *Ilizwe lamaFama*, organising some 5,000 farmers in some 44 villages. When we looked at the rural development chapter and discussed it with this group, *Ilizwe lamaFama*, they were saying: but it addresses none of the things that we were consulted on in the 2005 Land Summit. So, that is just one example of perhaps a consultation process that the NPC took but that was fostering and engineering consensus at a particular level of society without a real popular process of participation.

I will not go through the question of policy assumptions, which I think Professor Vusi Gumede has covered to an extent. Now, having put forward all these critiques, what then do I put forward in conclusion as some elements that could contribute to what is absolutely needed: a society that talks to itself and solves its problems. I am thinking of this in structural terms. Can the unemployed and workers build structural power to introduce what is an absolutely important, absolutely essential mass dynamic in recasting the power matrix? Can we harness the dissent and restlessness that we see to a new power that is conscious in a way that creates uncertainty for Comrade Trevor; in a way that creates uncertainty for the captains of industry? I'm not talking about uncertainty in a negative way. Again, I'm drawing on Habib where he makes the point that in South-East Asia, the elites were able to fashion certain processes of development, simply because there were a range of objective factors that forced them to take some options. He called it uncertainty. Can we build mass movements out of the restlessness? We're not there yet. We just see restlessness, which does not then produce effective processes of mass empowerment. If we are to do that, I think there are a number of tasks to take into account: critical political consciousness.

In this regard then, when you have got sufficiently organised forces on the ground, which have got critical consciousness, then they are able to engage smartly, effectively with economic policy debates beyond rhetoric and in ways that then really transform local spaces. We're very far from that. Can we have systems, approaches of sustained mass participatory organising? That is absolutely crucial for me. What unions have done, what the so-called social movements have done, fall far short in this regard. We have been able to move people into action to express anger: that's just limited mobilisation. It's not sustained organising that builds power so that actually what you can talk about is a social force with a social weight, with a strategy and a programme. So for me, if we are to bring change into the dynamic of social dialogue, that is the absolutely crucial task facing those of us who are activists in various ways.

In conclusion, I'm not being a sceptic who rejects social dialogue, negotiations, bargaining, in a crude way. The balance of forces requires that those must happen. In any case, as Professor Fioramonti was saying, all of us, whether we're capitalist or socialist, are concerned about what happens to this country. But then, what is absent in my view is an understanding or a conceptualisation of the process of social dialogue that shapes the balance of power in favour of workers and the poor. We're very far from that. I think, if we are to address that, we have to build in very effective structural leverages for the workers and the poor.

PART 4

INNOVATION AND TRANSDISCIPLINARY KNOWLEDGE FOR ACTION

Twenty-first century sustainability depends much on integrated knowledge development and application. The prism used since the industrial revolution, of discipline-focused research and training, has become problematic and requires a paradigm shift. The inadequacy of old methods of approaching complex problems is becoming more and more obvious. Critically, interconnected crises such as climate change, growing inequality and social anomie, transnational health pandemics, and threats of terrorism, require strategic and integrated long-term solutions. It seems clear that research and education should move from multidisciplinarity to transdisciplinarity. What balance should be struck between, for instance, high-level, high-risk research and the demand, from industry and governments, for immediate practical solutions to current challenges? For middle-income countries in the South, is there ideological space to grow, nurture and support blue-sky research whose immediate results may not be directly apparent? What measures can be mobilised to reverse the African brain drain? What needs to be done to empower indigenous knowledge systems or communities of practices beyond politically correct courtesies?

Innovation and Transdisciplinary Knowledge for Action – Tshilidzi Marwala

When I was given this topic 'Innovation and Transdisciplinarity' I thought it was quite a difficult topic because innovation is something that we probably do not know how to accurately measure and, therefore, it becomes very difficult to be able to quantify it. How innovation links to transdisciplinarity is even more complicated. I must also say that I do have a problem with the concept of transdisciplinarity, because I do know many disciplines that are actually transdisciplinary. For example, when we teach engineers we have to teach them sociology. So engineering is not a discipline but a transdiscipline. We have to teach engineering students mathematics, management and engineering courses.

So I am going to try to link transdisciplinarity to innovation. How do we measure innovation? I think there are a few key items that you can track in order to measure innovation. One of them is the number of publications. If we assume that what is being published is original, then it is innovative by definition and that is what many countries, including the OECD, use to measure the degree of innovation within a particular country. Or you can measure the number of patents and it has become very fashionable these days to measure patents. A patent is basically a right to use the commercial value of an idea.

So in my talk, I am going just to give you a picture of where we are when it comes to innovation as a country and as a continent and how we compare with the rest of the world. Then, I am going to end with answering some of the key questions that have been put forward to me.

Now let's just look at the number of publications, and I'm just going to assess Africa as a whole using the Scopus database. In this regard, we publish in a period of five years about 300,000 publications as the African continent, and these are cited almost a million times and we have about 276,000 authors and we publish 18 per cent in medicine. I must add here that, in medicine, it is normally people in the West who are doing clinical studies on the continent, who come to Africa, and then the publications are reflected here because there are also local collaborators. This picture does tell us something: that when it comes to the issue of science and technology we are not as dynamic as we would like to be.

Now if we look at these disciplines, quite a number of them are transdisciplinary. For example, medicine: we all know that when you go and study medicine it is a field that evolves from many disciplines coming together including science, biology, sociology and statistics. Now if we look at where we as a continent actually are as compared to the rest of the world, 9.2 per cent of the publications actually come from Africa, and 12.2 per cent of those would be in what we call the top journals. In terms of collaboration, almost half of our publications, 45.8 per cent, are collaborated; and again it tells us that most of these ideas or innovations, whichever way you want to call them, actually are coming from outside, and the collaboration index tells us exactly that.

Now if we just look at where we publish the most as the continent, medicine comes top because of clinical studies. Agricultural and biological sciences also feature prominently because there are many countries that, as part of their strategy, have identified Africa as a source of their security of supply of food production. We read stories, for example, of China buying land in Ethiopia so that they can be able to use it for agricultural purposes.

I'm not going to go through everything in detail, but a picture is actually emerging as to whether we are the source of innovation or we are actually importing innovation. Rather than importing innovation, are we just a platform for innovation to happen and then it is exported to the rest of the world?

Now let's look at South Africa: the same picture emerges. Around 79,000 publications emanate from South Africa and were cited 382,000 times; that is, the utilisation of those publications. You can see the distribution of the fields is more balanced than on the continent. For example, medicine is only 15.9 per cent, whereas before, on the continent, it was higher.

In South Africa, 12.8 per cent of the publication outputs are in the top journals, and the international collaboration is 44 per cent. This picture in South Africa is slightly different from the rest of the continent.

In South Africa, some of the collaborations actually emanate in South Africa, where South African academics initiate the collaboration, whereas if you analyse the continent, overall, the collaborations are initiated elsewhere and the trend still looks the same with medicine at the top. The amount of money that goes to the top earner of money for research from outside due to clinical trials in one university is about R600 million. This is research on testing medicines by pharmaceutical companies and finds its way into publications.

Now if we compare ourselves as a continent, how do we fare? This is really the ranking in terms of research productivity or innovation, if you would like to put it that way. South Africa is top, followed by Egypt, and then followed by Nigeria, then by Tunisia, then by Algeria, then Morocco, then Kenya, then Ethiopia, then Uganda, then Ghana, then Tanzania, then Cameroon, then Senegal and then Zimbabwe. Nigeria has a population which is close to three times our population so they are obviously not performing at their optimal level.

It's one thing coming up with an innovative idea; it's another for that innovative idea to be used. For example, I can go and apply for a patent for a six-legged chair, but is it useful and does it have commercial value?

Then, if we compare ourselves with the BRICS nations, you can see from the total output that the usual suspects emerge as leading in this front. For example, China is producing much higher than any one of us, and it is followed by India, a distant second, then followed by Brazil, then followed by Russia, then followed by South Africa. In fact, China is almost neck-and-neck with the United States, which has been dominating this index for quite a while.

Then the citations: don't be surprised when you see the deterioration from one year to another. Obviously, if you come up with an idea in 2009, and measure it today, it will have been utilised more frequently than an idea that you came up with yesterday; so the older the idea, the more the utilisation. When we go for field-weighted statistics, South Africa is doing well. We are obviously weighted to the size of our economy and all other factors.

Now when we talk about collaboration, China actually is almost last. It's very interesting. They produce the most output but they collaborate the least in the BRICS system. What does this mean? It basically tells you about the internal capacity of China: that they are able to do a great deal of research on their own. Collaboration is not bad, but if for every project or innovation that you have to do you have to collaborate then there is a problem. There has to be a mix that we really need to look at; and then, in terms of top percentile journals, South Africa is doing well.

Now what are the key questions that we really need to answer today? Is there a relationship between transdisciplinarity and innovation? Of course there is a relationship. You couldn't come up with social network software unless you understand computer science and sociology, for example. Are our curricula geared towards transdisciplinarity? Maybe not as much as what we see in North America where people in the sciences are required to read social sciences and humanities at much greater levels than we do. And part of the reason is funding, because if you were just to open up and say that, if you are studying computer science, 10 per cent of your courses must be in the humanities, it would actually be quite chaotic given our staff-to-student ratio. The staff-to-student ratio is actually a bottleneck.

Then the other question that we need to answer is: should we view government, academia and industry as a system – because we are not operating as a system? The problems that we are trying to solve in academia are not necessarily the problems that are linked to the government's agenda. I know that the National Research Foundation tries to do that but, if you go and just take a look at what is happening in South Africa, you realise that sometimes we even solve problems that are not necessarily our problems. So we should find a mechanism through which we view government, academia and industry as a system. We don't even meet that often. We don't have an annual meeting where government, academia and society come together and plan together.

How do we ensure that we solve local problems rather than global problems? How do we do that? Because when you have a young person, for his standing to actually rise, he has to solve global problems. There is a belief that, if you solve local problems, you will not necessarily publish or go and write patents in the USA. So how do we balance that? And how do we fund it? At the end of the day it comes to funding.

How do we balance basic versus applied research? It's quite clear that basic research is very, very expensive and much of it is in dreamland. It's something in which the probability that it will be used is lower than applied research, because in applied research you go and look at the problems people are facing and then you go and craft research problems to solve those problems. And I think that is another thing that we really need to work on.

I will end up by talking about the brain drain. How do we stem Africa's brain drain? I was talking to a professor from Delaware here and he was telling me that the dean of the engineering faculty is from Nigeria. You know, it's part of the brain drain and I think we should be open-minded about it, such as visiting scholar programmes. You don't have to be here because you can't control the ambitions of people, but you can create a system where they can be able to contribute. The infrastructure is one issue, because some of these people leave because they are following the infrastructure. Programmes such as the Square Kilometre Array (SKA) are obviously going to assist. We must have more of that. With regard to collaboration, we should have funding instruments that are directed at Africans living abroad. Countries that have benefited quite greatly are Australia and Canada. Apparently, when you go to some towns you only see South Africans. So for those who have left, we have to create mechanisms through which we can still be able to engage them in a much more active manner. And then technology is very important because we can use technology to make sure that, even when people leave, we still have much to do with them.

Intellectual Discourse on Transdisciplinarity –
Hester du Plessis

Abstract

The question posed for this session was whether South Africa has the ideological space to grow, nurture and support 'blue-sky research'. Though the enquiry is focused on the possible existence of the ideological space in question, the intellectual impact of researchers on the relationship between science and society is probably as significant as that of any ideological space.

To avoid getting lost in the vast academic landscape required to attend to this question in a scholarly manner, this paper will narrow down the focus to one specific area of change that was witnessed during the past twenty years: the dynamic relationship that developed between science and society. Popularly referred to as the 'science and society paradigm', this relationship is built on four conceptual pillars:

- The nature and application of Mode Two production of knowledge.
- The contextualisation of knowledge in a new (and constantly evolving) public space.
- New and favourable conditions for the production of socially robust knowledge.
- Socially distributed expertise bringing together science communicators, the media and museum specialists (Nowotny, *et al.* 2001).

The paper will explore the contributions that are made by intellectuals as well as specific fields of research that enable a transdisciplinary approach to research within the science and society paradigm.

Introduction

The academic landscape is continuously evolving and new findings and ideas are constantly being absorbed. When C. P. Snow (1959) alerted us to epistemological divides that exist between the Sciences and Humanities, a measure of discomfort entered the academic world regarding the way we communicate and share research. When Thomas Kuhn (1962) proposed that paradigms and paradigm shifts constantly influence the way we think, we were able to recognise dominant areas of knowledge production as well as identify the development of new intellectual domains. It was, however, only when Basarab Nicolescu (1996) alerted us to the restriction we enforce on the development of ideas through disciplinary-bound research, that our world opened up to the limitations of knowledge production processes and findings. This was when we started to embrace the idea of a transdisciplinary approach to research.

Helga Nowotny (2001) pointed out that, in the present, rapidly transforming society, we find it increasingly difficult to differentiate between the domains of the state and the market, culture and mass media and public and private arenas. Michael Gibbons (1984: 19) informed us that ' … the production of knowledge is advancing into a new phase. It operates according to new imperatives in tension with the traditional way of doing things with far-reaching implications'. Instead of knowledge being produced in a disciplinary-based academic framework (Mode One of knowledge production), there is now acknowledgement for the transdisciplinary production of knowledge (Mode Two), which is characterised by a continuous flow between fundamental and applied knowledge – between the theoretical and the practical.

Within the framework of Mode Two, new knowledge is produced where existing theories are put to use and where the results lead to new theories. In this manner, human resources become more mobile and research becomes more flexible. Michael Gibbons' (1984) proposed Mode One and Mode Two systems of knowledge production created a stir amongst science researchers with its shift towards a transdisciplinary approach and placed 'uncertainty' central within (consumer-driven) science investigations.

Similarly, the market (economy) is changing through the erosion of public-service ethics and the state is at present acting as a mere facilitator of the market. The market, in its own right, is becoming increasingly insubstantial and metaphorical. The 'market label' is progressively being used as a marker for social, political and cultural activities – implicating virtual products far removed from identifiable economic arenas.

These changes are also happening with culture. Culture and politics have merged and culture has become commoditised as a political tool. It is inevitable that the way we communicate is also changing. Characterised by the rapid development of communication technology, we are witnessing a so-called 'global participation explosion' – something that is essential for the development and support of sustainable democracy.

Some of these 'new' communication activities are identified by Edna Einsiedel (2008: 173) as: 'citizen involvement', 'stakeholder engagement', 'participatory technology assessment', 'indigenous people's rights', 'local community consultation', 'NGO intervention', 'multi-stakeholder dialogue', 'access to information' and 'access to justice'. Einsiedel (2008: 174) further listed three priority conditions that should underpin public participation:

- access to information;
- participation in decision-making; and
- judicial redress (where necessary).

In order to reflect on the need for a reformulation of 'public participation', we need to investigate the foundations of 'information', 'qualification' and 'participation'. We could pose two strategic issues for consideration when repositioning the role of communication within a modern transformed political and cultural domain:

- ideology in the conceptualisation of the state and its impact on the public sphere; and
- the postcolonial governance system in South Africa, illustrating the differences in the democratic struggle for ideological freedom.

The first issue requires understanding of the kind of ideology we are talking about. In this regard, many postcolonial examples exist within Africa of efforts to follow specific political ideologies in order to decolonise Africa. For example, numerous efforts were made to institute an African socialism that manifested itself in many forms over the past decades. We find that the African ideological spectrum ranges from a ' … more or less pure Marxism-Leninism to populist ideas rather similar to the Russian narodiks or Gandhi in India, as well as nationalist ideology' (Hettne, 1995: 85). Some mixed ideological perspectives used in the African past included:

- The Afro-Marxist emphasised Marxist-Leninist ideas of economic development and political structure. Major examples were Kwame Nkrumah (Ghana) and Sekou Touré (Guinea) during the first half of the 1960s.

- The moderate socialists, including Jomo Kenyatta (Kenya) and Kenneth Kaunda (Zambia), favoured a state-controlled 'socialist' economy but were at the same time anxious to attract foreign investment capital.
- The social democrats were closely connected with European socialism and frequently followed a pro-Western outlook, for example Leopold Senghor (Senegal) and Tom Mboya (Kenya).
- The agrarian-socialists (populists) were associated with Julius Nyerere's (Tanzania) Ujamaa-philosophy. Rather than looking for foreign models of socialism, Nyerere looked for it in traditional African society (Klinghoffer 1969: 16).

The main force behind the popular developmentalist ideology prevalent in Africa has been nationalism, urging the nation to draw level with developed countries. However, ' ... by the 1990s the African state has become the most demonised institution in Africa, vilified for its weaknesses, its over-extension, its interference with the smooth functioning of the markets, its repressive character, its dependence on foreign powers, its ubiquity, its absence, etc. It is now the "rentier state", the "over-extended state", the "parasitical state", the "predatory state", the "lame Leviathan state", the "patrimonial state", the "prebendal state", the "crony state", the "kleptocratic state", etc.' (Mkandawire, 2011).

An increasing number of African states are at present grappling with the idiosyncrasies of democracy in its various forms. Signs of multi-party politics and fraud-free elections are sometimes few and far between: ' ... the number of full "electoral democracies" among the 49 sub-Saharan countries has fallen from 24 in 2005 to 19 today ... but setting aside the quality of African democracy, all but a few of the continent's one billion people now expect to vote in regular national polls. That is something which 1.5 billion Asians, for all their impressive economic performance, cannot do (*The Economist*, 31 March 2012).'

To create space to grow, nurture and support blue-sky research, and to find a foothold within academia, is often difficult within these dominant and often hybrid ideologies. To broaden our understanding of the possibility for blue-sky research we need to shift attention beyond political ideologies. One example would be to look at the relation between science and society and efforts to communicate science within the public domain.

The Relationship Between Science and Society

The current dominant science communication paradigm is that of 'science and society'. The science and society paradigm created space for an intensified debate around the most appropriate and applicable science communication model for the effective functioning of Science Communication and Public Understanding of Science (PUS) research. In this regard there is ongoing debate, specifically from the social sciences, regarding the continued application of the deficit model that was originally adopted to drive European-based survey processes and reporting. The deficit model is globally recognised as a dominant framework for science communication processes.

The relationship between science and society is both complex and complicated. New and powerful technologies are sometimes unconditionally considered as a blessing to uplift the way we live. The rapid growth in knowledge means that we are increasingly dealing with things we do not understand that demand new ways of thinking about the way we live. According to Paul Cilliers (1998), these new challenges require philosophy to play a more important role by being an integral part of scientific and technological practice. We now realise that science and society cannot be planned in a premeditated manner and that nature is not simply acting on cause and effect. The current intellectual move beyond disciplinary boundaries initiated innovative and complex thinking, the possibility to expand our 'ways of knowing' (epistemology) and the generation of new knowledge.

To get to grips with complexity, the transdisciplinary approach to research is a solution to bridge the divide between science and society by bringing together multiple science-based actors to reflect collaboratively on scientific inventions and their effects on society. Of course the opposite is also true: society is playing a more pronounced role in directing scientific research. We are witnessing that the state, as a modern political entity with its promise of technological efficiency, is showing cracks and is becoming incapable of keeping up with the rapid pace of scientific development. Society, citizens and the public(s) are actively participating in ever-growing numbers in evaluating the value of science and it is now impossible to ignore the impact of social movements and the causes they take up.

The Conference Debate

The popular endeavour of this year's reflection on the past twenty years of democracy in South Africa is to measure our material progress (economics) and physical well-being (education and health). In the wake of developments around the science and society paradigm, we also find (though less emphasised) a growing association with the rapid growth in our intellectual understanding of the constant metamorphosis of social and political ideas. Two domains are challenged: that of the 'scientific-economic' and that of the 'socio-political', promoting a demand for new economic models and new socio-political terms – driven by the reconceptualisation of old perceptions and practices.

Within the perspective of the science and society paradigm, we need to take into account a number of new options that can only be considered under blue-sky research. For example, as argued by Masao Miyoshi in *Trespasses* (2010), two social paradigms currently confront us: that of intellectuals and their specialisations and that of nations and their exiles. In the case of South Africa, both aspects profoundly affect the production of knowledge (as subject) and the forging of a new identity as a nation (as object). These meta-narratives, we assume, have resumed their position as central to knowledge production where it is no longer possible to ignore meta-topics (such as society and climate change) without the assistance of the 'science and society' model.

Transformation in the Production of Knowledge

We have already followed the argument that the production of knowledge has witnessed radical changes over the past twenty years. Not only did academic disciplines grow in number, but the underlying thirst for knowledge is transforming our ways of acquiring knowledge in both scope and intent. One of these is the move towards joint problem solving amongst and between the disciplines. Joint problem solving increased the necessity to integrate perspectives on the identification, formulation and resolution of shared problems. As a result, we have now entered a world of complexity whereby ideas, as argued by Paul Cilliers (1998), can be analysed separately and then put together again.

Recognition of the role of complexity in knowledge production quickly led to the realisation that we cannot conclude that, once dissected, the sum of the components of the idea will remain the same when 'put together again'. New knowledge spaces opened up to form new relationships between the different parts. Coupled with our growing inability to fully understand the complexity of science, technology and society we are turning to blue-sky research (in the social sciences and the humanities) to help us: firstly to identify global meta-narratives and secondly to guide the local new relationships we experience during recent (transformative) times.

The Intellectuals

Both the range and scope of new knowledge gained from a transdisciplinary approach have emerged as an important, exciting and challenging domain. Two changes may be worth mentioning. The growing number of recent publications on the topic of 'being an intellectual' reflects the interest in self-discovery, claim of identity and also self-critique. It is well understood how the apartheid system divided cultures and built a divisive intellectual history – mostly based on the supposed supremacy of the West against the Rest. With the end of apartheid this intellectual legacy was challenged, its normative base called suspect and its theories of intellectual supremacy discredited. It was clear that a new understanding of our 'ways of thinking' was required. Keeping in mind that this is an elusive ideal that lacks any form of preordained framework, we had to embark on a collective exploration of the fit and purpose of ideas to assist us in understanding our new-found freedom and what value our collective knowledge might add.

With the examination of ideas being crucial in understanding the underlying issues that constitute the formation of a nation, the role of the intellectual has therefore grown in importance. We see this by the growing list of publications reflecting on the role of the intellectual over the past twenty years. These publications range from examining the diverse intellectual traditions in South Africa (Vale, P. and Hamilton, L. and Prinsloo, H. 2014. *Intellectual Traditions in South Africa: Ideas, Individuals and Institutions.* Scottsville: University of KwaZulu-Natal Press) to blaming the intellectuals for 'being in retreat' (Gumede, W. & Dikeni, L. 2009. *The Poverty of Ideas: South African Democracy and the Retreat of Intellectuals.* Auckland Park: Jacana). A welcome addition to this growing lexicon of publications is the introduction of previously unrecognised intellectuals as well as recent debates found in Bjorn Beckman and Gbemisola Adeoti. 2006. *Intellectuals and African Development: Pretensions and Resistance in African Politics.* Senegal: CODESRIA.

Most importantly, we find individual academic contributions in the field of philosophy improving our understanding of ideas within a South African and African context. The introduction to philosophical thinking, produced by P. H. Coetzee and A. P. J. Roux: *Philosophy from Africa*. (2002). Pretoria: Unisa, serves as example.

Transdisciplinarity

There is growing awareness that the application of a transdisciplinary approach to research is integral to the way African societies function and think. This is captured by the late Dani Nabudere (2012. *Afrikology and Transdisciplinarity: A Restorative Epistemology*. Pretoria: AISAs). While exploring the restriction inherent to the concept of restorative justice on the African continent in its relation to international humanitarian law, Nabudere argues that disciplinary boundaries inhibit our capabilities of looking at realities in a comprehensive way. Hence the 'restorative approach' has become a major global social movement and, applied in Africa, this has become a way to restore, establish, identify and ensure a sense of dignity and security in Africa after years of political and military subjugation of societies.

For Nabudere, it became clear that a fragmented world-view leads to misunderstanding and problems within society. Fragmented knowledge production (as found in disciplinary specialisation) originated from the different (sometimes competing) paradigms represented by the natural sciences, social sciences and the humanities, with the divisions often leading to conceptual mismatches and misunderstandings. How, then, do we enable great ideas to help us formulate a national identity and enter the corridors of government as directives for good governance?

The MISTRA Project on Transdisciplinarity

In an attempt to answer this difficult question, MISTRA introduced a research project studying the intellectual application of a transdisciplinary approach to research. MISTRA, at the same time, adopted transdisciplinarity as a guiding institutional principle. In this context, MISTRA published a book: du Plessis, H. and Sehume, J. and Martin, L. 2013. *The Concept and Application of Transdisciplinarity in Intellectual Discourse and Research*. Johannesburg: Real African Publishers.

The study aimed to comprehend the principles and specific attributes of Mode Two knowledge production that are central to the development of a transdisciplinary approach to research. The first understanding is that the intent of research has shifted to practical application (Gadamer's hermeneutics). Secondly, hyper-specialisation has become limiting in the quest for heterogeneity of skills necessary to ensure application (challenging the hierarchical and disciplinary-based systems still prevalent at many universities). The third attribute is to apply a transdisciplinary approach in order to present a different intellectual focus. In this way, transdisciplinarity becomes an attempt at formulating an integrative process of knowledge production and distribution (in reaction against the twentieth century occurrence of narrow discipline focus and hyperspecialisation). It directly responds to complex and multilayered challenges, such as diffused disciplines, interlinked socio-economic problems, impacts of globalisation, de-territorialised nation states, technological advancements, environmental concerns, food security and much more.

Transdisciplinarity recognises the complex character of realities that calls for more than one discipline in terms of interpretation and application. It acknowledges the need for joint problem solving mechanisms and seeks to stimulate unification of knowledge paradigms. It is concerned with cross-fertilisation of experiences and skills by providing a road to a convergence of expertise. A key factor is that, even though knowledge is complex and multidimensional, there is firstly a possibility of unity in this complexity and, secondly, practical unity of action.

In the context of the meta-narrative, transdisciplinarity is central to the effort to address the big question at the heart of the so-called global 'civilisational project'. Doing research on civilisations embraces controversy. Whether research focuses on West/East, primitive/civilised or ancient/modern, it remains a problematic area that requires reflexive thinking and radical responses to the binaries with which it has been associated. Bridging the gap between the disciplines provides opportunity for shared knowledge that reaches beyond the restricted sphere of disciplinary-bound application of knowledge.

Transdisciplinarity is, therefore, by orientation, an approach that recognises a united and borderless intellectual initiative. It proposes an integrative process of knowledge production and dissemination through the following steps:

- It firstly follows a method that recognises the *ontological axiom*: what we encounter in nature and in our knowledge of nature brings recognition for the existence of different levels of reality and different levels of perceptions.
- Secondly, it positions a *logical axiom*: the passage from one level of

reality to another that is ensured by the logic of the included middle.

- Thirdly, we find the *complexity axiom* that forms the structure of the totality of levels of reality or perception and as complex structure: every level is what it is because all the levels exist at the same time (Nicolescu, 1996).

The Healing of the Nation?

To return to Masao Miyoshi's two important leading social paradigms (*Trespasses*, 2010): that of intellectuals and their specialisations and that of nations and their exiles. The role of the intellectual, the intellectual in exile, and local narratives are crucial to understanding the meta-narrative guiding complex topics such as nationhood, values and worldviews. In the past twenty years, South Africa enjoyed renewed intellectual vigour while re-entering the international academic arena. At the same time, exiles returned with knowledge that added significant value to the local 'ways of knowing' (epistemology) and assisted us to develop a global consciousness. We all come from a past that was characterised by censorship (who still remembers that the works of Frantz Fanon were banned?) and acquiescence (blaming the West for imposing knowledge).

Our understanding of the complexity between 'science and society' is underdeveloped and in need of intensified debate through public engagement. The question arises: how do we move beyond nostalgia about our own personal (struggle) past, avoid being utopian about our relatively new democracy, and cope with a world where society is under growing pressure to handle international forces? Do we conform or transform? Transnational (multinational) corporations do not depend on the nation state of their origin for protection and facilitation since they reside outside of nation state structures. Are our intellectuals prepared to participate and become the apologists for transnational corporatism?

Conclusion

As Masao Miyoshi states: 'With the demise of authoritarian socialist states, bourgeois capitalism looked as if it had triumphed over all rivals … the disappearance of "the other side" together with the end of administrative colonialism, has placed the nation state in a vacant space that is ideologically uncontested and militarily constabulised.' Will we continue to blindly follow rulers from dominant corporate structures with their low regard for societal needs and interests? The answer is simple: we need to support efforts to bring science and society into intense dialogue within the public domain and we need to adopt a transdisciplinary approach to enable us to fully understand all the factors and uncertainties that we are about to encounter.

The science and society paradigm possibly offers the best solution to engage with the public: the European Commission's *Monitoring Policy and Research Activities on Science in Society in Europe* (MASIS) 2012 report (www.masis.eu) considers the 'science in society' paradigm in Europe to be dominated by issues related to its role in sustainable development as well as to the appropriate governance of science. Most significantly, the MASIS report states: 'Discussions and processes relating to the appropriateness of science in society should be inclusive and based on broad public and stakeholder engagement' ... since ... 'societal challenges can only be tackled if society is fully engaged in science, technology and innovation ... it should be stressed that the dynamics of public and stakeholder engagement remains an important object for further research and experimentations.'

References

Cilliers, Paul. 1998. *Complexity and Postmodernism: Understanding Complex Systems.* London: Routledge.

Coetzee, P. H. 2002. *Philosophy from Africa.* Cape Town: Oxford University Press.

du Plessis, H. and Sehume, J. and Martin, L. 2013. *The Concept and Application of Transdisciplinarity in Intellectual Discourse and Research.* Johannesburg: Real African Publishers.

Einsiedel, Edna. 2008. 'Public participation and dialogue'. In: Bucchi, M. and Trench, B. *Handbook of Public Communication of Science and Technology.* London: Routledge.

Gibbons, M. & Gummett, P. (eds.) 1984. *Science, Technology and Society Today.* Manchester: Manchester University Press.

Hettne, B. 1995. *Development Theory and the Three Worlds.* Essex: Longman.

Klinghoffer, A. J. 1969. *Soviet Perspectives on African Socialism.* Cranbury, NJ: Rutherford/Fairleigh Dickenson University Press.

Kuhn, T. 1962. *The Structure of Scientific Revolutions.* Chicago: University of Chicago Press.

Miyoshi, Masao. 2010. *Trespasses.* Durham and London: Duke University Press.

Nicolescu, Basarab. 1996. *La transdisciplinarité, Manifeste.* Paris: Éditions du Rocher.

Nicolescu, Basarab. 1996. 'Levels of complexity and levels of reality'. In: Pullman, B. 1996. *The Emergence of Complexity in Mathematics, Physics, Chemistry and Biology.* Vatican City, Pontificia Academia Scientiarum. Distributed by Princeton University Press. Proceedings of the plenary session of the Pontifical Academy of Sciences, pp. 27–31, October 1992, Casino Pio IV, Vatican.

Nicolescu, Basarab. 2002. *Manifesto of Transdisciplinarity*, translated from the French by Karen-Claire Voss. New York: SUNY.

Nicolescu, Basarab. 2008. (ed.) *Transdisciplinarity: Theory and Practice*. New Jersey: Hampton.

Nowotny, Helga 'The Potential of Transdisciplinarity'. http://www.interdisciplines.org/interdisciplinarity/papers/5/printable/paper [Accessed: 2007/08/13].

Nowotny, Helga and Scott, Peter and Gibbons, Michael. 2001. *Re-thinking Science: Knowledge and the Public in an Age of Uncertainty*. London: Polity.

Snow, C. P. 1959 [1998]. The Two Cultures. Cambridge: Cambridge University Press.

The Economist. 2012. 'African democracy: a glass half-full. Representative government is still on the march in Africa, despite recent hiccups', 31 March. Available at: <http://www.economist.com/node/21551494>

Innovation and Transdisciplinary Knowledge for Action –
Erika Kraemer-Mbula

In this short intervention I will try to arrive to one point, which is the importance of adopting a systemic perspective when we think about generating the type of skills, knowledge and new ideas that we need to face the multiple and complex challenges of our time.

We are in a unique moment in history, in which there is an apparent need to evolve in the way we understand innovation, knowledge generation, knowledge use and diffusion. The magnitude and complexity of current developmental issues has become evident. Firstly, we are currently operating beyond our planetary boundaries. We have reached and passed the tipping point of many of our ecological and natural systems, bringing a future shaped by severe uncertainties. The effects of the speed of change and the connections of these changes with human systems are still unknown to us. We certainly need a much better understanding of the implications that moving beyond those planetary boundaries will have in our survival and well-being.

Secondly, current modes of production and consumption are largely unsustainable. Productive systems in both industrialised and less industrialised countries are not taking sufficient advantage of global advances in 'cleaner' technologies. This is particularly worrying in the context of Africa, where population is expected to double in the next decade, putting unprecedented pressure on our social and geographical environments, such as urban areas.

Thirdly, our social and economic environments are characterised by growing inequalities at many different levels, globally, within nations and between regions, as well as in terms of income and social inequalities. This makes us interrogate how sustainable certain livelihoods are. For instance, a large part of the employment generated in South Africa and Africa is generated in the informal economy; however, the informal economy remains out of consideration in discussions related to education, training, skills development and innovation. How do we link our socio-economic reality to the issue of inter- and transdisciplinarity?

Sustainability and equitability are increasingly identified in academic and policy spheres as major challenges for the future. This has manifested in the ongoing transition from millennium development goals (MDGs) to the sustainable development goals (SDGs). Generating the type of knowledge needed to face these challenges clearly requires a much more bottom-up, locally-based, trans- and interdisciplinary type of expertise, as well as benefiting from the solutions that technological advances have made available to us. However, it is not all bad news, since evidence also shows us that the African continent as a whole, and South Africa in particular, are improving their performance in terms of education and research outputs.

So we have decreasing levels of illiteracy across Africa but we also have challenges in terms of low-quality basic education in terms of science and maths. Enrolment in tertiary education has doubled in Africa in the last seven years or so, and we see a proliferation of public and private universities, as well as training organisations. We also see that the production of academic knowledge is skewed towards the humanities and social sciences and some have argued that we don't have enough science, technology, engineering and maths (STEM) capabilities.

In sub-Saharan Africa, research outputs have doubled but still our global share is very small considering that we have twelve per cent of the global population. Moreover, research is still heavily reliant on international funding. South Africa is an outlier in Africa, and generates about 85 per cent of the research output in southern Africa. South Africa's research performance stands out in the region as well as on the continent, not only in terms of quantity, but also the quality of research in terms of citation impact, which has moved from below the world average to over the world average in the last ten years.

South Africa also has the largest share of science, technology, engineering and maths (STEM) related research outputs. So how do we reconcile the advances in education and research that we are experiencing, not only in South Africa but broadly on the continent, with the expanding challenges that lie ahead of us? I will try to give some thoughts about how to fit these two together and what are the implications they have for interdisciplinarity and transdisciplinarity.

Some of the limitations that we experience here in South Africa relate to the concentration of these advances in research capabilities. Advances are not widespread across the whole higher education system or research system, but in a few universities. In view of this concentration, questions have been raised about local relevance of university research – how can research activities connect with a broader range of stakeholders? Also, the argument has been raised that South Africa's research system is not sufficiently well connected to other sub-regional systems of innovation and here we can think about the southern African region as well: how does South Africa's research system relate to its neighbouring countries? The answer is that there is plenty of room for collaboration, and many benefits to be gained.

Finally, I would like to discuss the importance of adopting a systemic view in terms of the production and use of knowledge. The innovation systems approach was generated a few decades ago as a reaction to a linear view of innovation that understood innovation as emerging almost exclusively from scientific research outputs generated in a university or a research organisation. An innovation systems approach considers innovation as something that emerges from the exchange and recombination of knowledge produced by a number of stakeholders. Not only universities, but also civil society, government organisations, research institutions, the private sector and so on.

So strengthening an innovation system implies improving the mechanisms for sharing knowledge. From an innovation systems perspective, interactions are central: it is not only about the performance of universities and the amount of research outputs, but more importantly about how they interact with the rest of the actors in the system. Without interactions there is no system. Without interactions we would just have isolated actors working in silos.

To conclude: what are the implications in terms of education and training under a systemic view of innovation? First of all, a broader understanding of skills development is required as something that happens not only in universities but in connection to the rest of the actors in the system. From a systemic perspective, there is an emerging need to generate interdisciplinary and transdisciplinary thinkers able to respond to the complex and multidimensional aspects of knowledge generation, dissemination and use, but able to apply that knowledge to address those grand challenges ahead of us. This requires strengthening, not only the first and the second missions of universities (teaching and research), but also the third mission of universities through research-based education and broader engagement with stakeholders. Now this is easier said than done and creating this type of transdisciplinary platform connecting academic experts, future researchers, policymakers, etc. on real topics, has been tried on various scales in other countries. Different modalities exist out there and now the question is: how do we adapt, adopt and domesticate these models to the context of South Africa?

South Africa's Democratic Transition and Transformation from 1994–2014: What Difference Has It Made to Date? – Mammo Muchie

Inspiration

Africa without South Africa can be like a ship without a captain; South Africa without the rest of Africa can be like a ship without a compass.
Mammo Muchie

South Africa Twenty Years after Apartheid?

As 2014 passes and 2015 comes, the twenty years of South African democracy is also entering the next twenty years, and beyond, and that is worth reflecting on. We have been captured by the South African anti-apartheid struggles throughout our lives. It is important that we continue to reflect on the way South Africa is navigating today and tomorrow the stormy waves of world politics and economics to transform the conditions of inherited injustice in South Africa itself. How strong is South Africa standing firmly to deal with all the internal and external challenges the country is facing today and tomorrow? Is South Africa playing the role of the captain with the rest of Africa as its compass to navigate the unpredictable waves of a difficult world? If not now, then when can it be welcomed to play a constructive role to help Africa emerge as its own leader in the coming centuries?!

We all know South Africa ended apartheid with a big compromise: where the formerly oppressed formally closed the historical chapter of the political fetters and rules that had fenced them into dispersed and divided Bantustan enclaves. This 'de-apartheid' freedom was earned with the formerly advantaged retaining still much of their economic privilege. Thus, to this day still, all South African citizens share political freedom without equally enjoying full economic justice. South African constitutional democracy appears to provide political freedom without fully realised economic justice, especially to the formerly racially-oppressed majority population.

The moral foundation of the struggle against apartheid was equality, end of repression, and justice, rather than revenge. Nelson Mandela was in jail unjustly for nearly a generation, to be precise, for 27 years, and was prepared, along with his comrades Oliver Tambo, Chris Hani, Thabo Mbeki and others, to go for reconciliation. (Sabelo J. Ndlovu-Gatsheni, 'From a "Terrorist" to Global Icon: A Critical Decolonial Ethical Tribute to Nelson Rolihlahla Mandela of South Africa', *Third World Quarterly*, 35(6), July 2014.) That was why the world was awed by the shining example of reconciliation and the embrace of the values of *ubuntu*.

In this commentary, we argue that the rainbow nation faces the challenging task of ensuring the economic and social justice that is necessary for the spirit and reality of political freedom to achieve its genuine meaning. This is important, not only for South Africa but also for the rest of the African continent, in that South Africa will not find itself in a strong position to engage the rest of Africa while its domestic economic landscape is dominated by excessive unemployment of the youth, inequality in income and opportunity, and not meeting ordinary citizens' expectations.

The plus side of this historic settlement is that it prevented the paradigm of war and launched South Africa into a constitutional democracy that has emerged as an example to the rest of the world for finding a peaceful way of handling what appeared to be an intractable protracted conflict. What makes 1994 a unique historical milestone is that war was replaced by peace, and reconciliation replaced conflict. The 'Rainbow nation of God' was born, according to Bishop Desmond Tutu. South Africa has now a morally radiant and intelligent global brand for ending conflict with peace and reconciliation. As Ethiopianism sustained the moral and spiritual call for independence from the yoke of colonialism throughout Africa and the colonised world, the struggle against apartheid and the reconciliation that followed set a new standard for justice and peace in the world.

Now the real challenge for South Africa is how to apply moral, emotional, political and social intelligence in order to build on the achievement of 1994 and innovate a new democratic synthesis by combining political democracy with economic justice; by avoiding once again any conflict; and by retaining and showcasing the country's distinguishing brand of a globally recognised moral standing.

There are tangible and recognised achievements over the last twenty years. Some of these are:

- commitment to and practice of vibrant democracy and political stability;
- improved access to education with more pupils going to schools at all levels;
- increased women's participation in the political process, with nearly 45 per cent of parliamentarians being women;
- an improved safety net (even though a lot more is to be desired): more housing units being built; an expansion of healthcare services; increased access to electricity, clean water and sanitation services;
- the integration of neighbourhoods and removal of racial 'group area' restrictions;
- stable macroeconomic conditions accompanied by declines of inflation rates to manageable single digits (as compared to double-digit inflation rates of the apartheid era of 1980–1994), and acceptable economic growth of an average of about 3.5 per cent (as compared to the 1.4 per cent of 1980–1994, during the last period of apartheid); and
- the existence of relatively high-quality institutions such as vibrant universities, vibrant media, decent courts, and a well-organised civil society (http://www.actsa.org/newsroom/wp-content/uploads/2014/05/South-Africa-20-years-of-Freedom-Achievements-and-Challenges.pdf).

The achievements are impressive, but there are also serious challenges: 'growing wealth and income disparities, high youth unemployment, labour unrest (which has led to the shutting down of some economic activities and even factories), and relative de-industrialization and dependence on commodity exports (Ibid.).'

The unfinished task is how to ensure equality of opportunity and economic mobility of the country's citizens and still retain the globally recognised and distinguished brand of moral standing. Pursuing the two grand objectives is a complex task and requires combining both the ideals of *ubuntu* and a shared collective commitment to create opportunities for the young generation to fully participate in the economic, social and political life of the rainbow nation.

But a warning: all South Africans, rich or poor, have to appreciate that democracy without economic justice for all will not be sustainable.

Democracy will be eroded if poverty, unemployment and inequality continue to rise, even if economic growth continues to take place. It depends on who continues to benefit and who continues to lose. The losers continue to be the historically disadvantaged majority. This has to change irreversibly now, twenty years on, and ways should be found to realise this and not just say it.

The real challenge for all South Africans is this: how to bring about and build on the successes of democratic practices by adding economic democracy, justice and freedom. That can only be achieved through a shared growth strategy and a concrete programme designed to help in reducing poverty, inequality and unemployment. Achieving those must be priorities for all South African stakeholders – private or public, university or community. This is human kindness – a dynamic society, economy and governance system anchored deeply in the values and principles of *ubuntu*. In reality, it is not much to ask for an economically and politically unified democracy, so that all South Africans can unite and rally behind and sustain the achievements of the last twenty years.

Economic and social transformation is a slow process, and yet, the last two decades have been too slow in bringing about economic democracy and in preparing the youth for the responsibilities and challenges of a fiercely competitive world. The indicators of inequality of income and opportunity across families and economic classes, the excessive unemployment rate of the youth, and the prevalence of poverty among historically repressed communities paint indeed an uncongenial if not depressing picture. There were several, but uncoordinated efforts, such as the Broad-based Black Economic Empowerment scheme (BBBEE), to address the challenge and these have not been effective or sustainable.

Inequality is growing even when South Africa has been reported to be the one country that has broken the global record in increasing the number of the richest percentage in the world: the number of millionaires has grown by 106 per cent over the last decade and multimillionaires by 102 per cent. That easily beats the global average of 58 per cent for millionaires and 71 per cent for multimillionaires. Africa is home to about 100,000 dollar millionaires – an increase of 7.4 per cent over the previous year. The number of Nigerian millionaires is expected to grow by 47 per cent over the next four years (*Africa Business*, no. 414, December 2014, p. 17).

The real challenge is not to increase the percentage of millionaires and multimillionaires with such concentration of ownership of wealth in South

Africa and the rest of Africa. It is how to make all citizens in South Africa, especially the previously underprivileged black majority, capable of leading a life of sustainable well-being with the provision of food, water, shelter, health, electricity and all basic necessities as part and parcel of the protection of the human rights of all.

The key challenge is to create a rainbow nation of full human rights, reflected in the removal of inequality, poverty and unemployment. It is how to use the success of the last twenty years of democracy to add economic democracy and social justice and create a South Africa where no one will be a beggar; no one starves; no one goes thirsty; everyone has decent shelter; no one is unemployed or unemployable; no one is poor and inequality is reduced; the Gini coefficient rather than growing is declining; and the society is anchored in deep values, norms, trust capital, networks and institutions. Democracy has to be anchored on the values and principles, norms and institutions that, above all else, prioritise the well-being of the people.

How can South Africa enliven and invigorate a dynamic society, economy and governance system anchored deeply in the values and principles of *ubuntu*? That is the real challenge that brooks no delay.

The key is to sustaining what emerged in 1994 by creating systematic interaction amongst the key factors that influence the well-being of people such as the intelligent and smart linkages between South Africa's economics with politics; the private with public sectors, the market with the state; the internal with external knowledge; the domestic technology creation with the transfer and exchange of external technology and knowledge; linking informal and formal sectors and linking strongly and consciously values from traditions like *ubuntu* with democracy that is associated with modernity. Not mimicry, but creativity, innovation, venture creation, social entrepreneurship and intelligence to guide the making of the future; not to think, learn and work hard, but to think, learn and work smartly, always with positive spirit – all this is the synergy that is critical to move the country forwards and onwards. Only when hard work is interlinked with working smartly can the political democracy that emerged in 1994 continue to make a socio-economic difference and improve people's lives, making what emerged as the post-apartheid era sustainable.

Suggestions for South Africa to Pursue in the Next Twenty Years

It is not good for any nation to be rich in goods and create a few millionaires relative to the population size with a world record and speed. It is more important to be rich in values, principles, ideas, norms, trust, institutions, spirituality and morality. We have nations that are materially very rich but are poor in providing spiritual public good. South Africa provided, in 1994, a spiritual public good with the arrangement to bring together those who were privileged with the majority who were underprivileged.

What is now essential in South Africa is to find resourceful ways to sustain the great historical moment that opened a democratic and free future for South Africans. That is to say, all should benefit, not just some.

In order to realise economic freedom, we recommend approaches that all South Africans can promote together to add to the current political democracy:

- vastly promote social entrepreneurship;
- promote science, technology, engineering, mathematics and innovation (STEMI);
- create, systematically, government-university-industry and civil society/community linkages;
- values of *ubuntu* for all (not just for South Africa, to save humanity too!);
- South African democracy with economic justice and freedom for promoting the African Renaissance; and
- the development of social, human and natural capital, not the pursuit of financial capital, should be seen as primary.

Infusing all in society with social entrepreneurship culture is to combine the following:

- compassion with competition;
- philanthropy with business;
- buy one to give one;
- buy what you need while giving to those in need;
- make profit with non-profit;
- economic gain with social gain;
- spend less, give more;
- doing good while doing good business;

- giving with selling;
- giving can serve as a brand for profit making; and
- charitable with growing the bottom line.

South Africa needs social entrepreneurs as much as new captains of industry and dynamic civil servants and university professors. Social entrepreneurship is the activity of establishing new business ventures to achieve social change, not just economic change. It is bringing economic change with social change and conversely social change with economic change: a win-win outcome. The business that combines social gain with economic gain can utilise creativity and innovation to bring social, financial, service, educational or other community benefits.

South Africa can promote better economic opportunities by promoting social entrepreneurs through building innovative partnerships: business, civil society, NGOs and committed individuals to deal with unequal economic conditions and challenges. South Africa can create an innovative culture of continuous transformation and reconciliation through the promotion of social entrepreneurial creative approaches to create a society based on social justice.

Promote Creativity and Innovation (STEMI)

Technical or innovative entrepreneurship is strictly science and technology based. But a science and technology system that creates technical or innovative entrepreneurs is still lacking, though South Africa is better in many ways than many other African states. The policy for science and technology needs to change, and the science and technology for improving policy needs to be streamlined and focused. South Africa needs intelligence for science, technology, engineering, mathematics and innovation (STEMI) as we do for intellect, politics, economics, emotions, morality and wisdom.

University, Government, Private and Community Interlinkages

What South Africa needs is to create productive power from kindergarten to tertiary levels by using STEMI to create domestic micro, small and medium-sized social entrepreneurial firms with a knowledge base.

Quality STEMI requires a functioning and sustainable training system. Quality STEMI is necessary for building national capability and competence and a skill and knowledge base. Such capability is necessary to enhance national productivity. National productivity, in turn, creates the knowledge, the trainees, inventions, innovations, patents and research outputs that can lead to application to meet social and economic objectives: i.e. to national utility contributing to community, society, economy and culture.

An integrated conception is needed to strongly develop the linkages, from quality to capability to productivity to utility (QCPU). This conception provides the basis for generating appropriate incentives. STEMI should be promoted creatively from kindergarten to university, ultimately to produce a graduate equipped with the knowledge, learning, innovation and competence (KLICs) throughout their lives, learning to invent, to innovate, and to design. The synergy of capability, productive power, human capital, social and mental capital is necessary to sustain a harmonious and innovative South Africa to make it also play an additional role as the pilot to help fly the rest of Africa to a bright future.

Ubuntu is a Heavenly Gift for South Africa

South Africa has a rare gift of *ubuntu*. All the institutions should collaborate to make *ubuntu* a way of life and an example for all. Values that are association-anchored – 'I am because you are' – and not calculative and instrumental that *ubuntu* promotes are so central to combining political democracy with social and economic democracy. South Africa can reinforce its 1994 morally radiant brand by promoting *ubuntu* across the world by its sheer power of practice of this value – the rich philosophy of 'there is an I in *You* and there is a *You* in I'.

South Africa for the African Renaissance

South Africa can promote the African Renaissance if its political democracy combines economic justice and freedom.

Social Capital Central to Sustain both Political and Economic Democracy

The briefest way to express social capital is to define it neatly and simply as trust capital. Trust is not easy to build, as it is not easy to sustain in any capitalist society. The market is built on pricing with the aim of valorising, above all else, profits. It is not easy to maintain trust even if it exists within such a system. Different values and economic realities need to exist to promote trust capital. If there is pervasive inequality, poverty, and unemployment, social capital will decline, crime will increase, and corruption, lying and cheating will prevail. 'I am not upset you lied to me; I am upset from now on I can't believe you (Friedrich Nietzsche).'

Social capital is built from such intangible matters as trust, norms, observance of rules and procedures in relationships, following principles, submitting to institutional logic and not to personalised and egoistic pursuits.

The building and the existence of social capital is a necessary condition to undertake sustainable transformation and development in any environmental, cultural and power context.

When the power of justice and ethics overcomes the love of power and money, the necessary condition for social capital to blossom will be firm.

Concluding Remarks

Over the last twenty years, in South Africa, we have seen wealth concentration and a high Gini coefficient, which are a danger to South Africa's constitutional democracy. If the wealthy keep piling up their wealth and the poor increase, a politics that plays on poverty will emerge naturally. Furthermore, political instability will also manifest through crime, corruption, industrial unrest and other social ills. The only way to sustain the democracy of these past twenty years is to address, in a unified approach, the eradication of poverty, unemployment, inequality, reduction in wealth concentration and ownership by the few by making the well-being of the majority the bedrock for the country's economic and social policy and development.

South Africa should create something like a community system of innovation, where the private sector, the university, community, civil society and different government sectors join to convert knowledge for stimulating grassroots innovation in the townships and rural areas.

South African stakeholders should consider a new synthesis that simultaneously promotes 'social entrepreneurship, STEMI, and the dynamic interlinkages of university, private, public, civil society and community'. This will help create a community-anchored innovation dynamic that will transform structurally the South African economic system.

The lesson here is that the constitutional democracy and political stability that has been built during the last twenty years will almost certainly be eroded if poverty, unemployment and inequality continue to rise: even if economic growth continues to take place. In other words, wealth maximisation without regard to reduction in inequality is a danger to the sustainability of South Africa's democracy.

Finally, when the task of redressing economic justice radiates like sunshine, South Africa's 1994 moral radiance will glow even brighter across the rest of Africa and the world. South Africa will become a **New Rainbow Nation and Civilisation of Equality, Full Employment and Eradication of Poverty.**

References

Africa Business No. 414, December 2014
(http://www.actsa.org/newsroom/wp- content/uploads/2014/05/South-Africa-20-years-of-Freedom- Achievements-and-Challenges.pdf

Landsberg, Chris. 2010. *The Diplomacy of Transformation: South African Foreign Policy and Statecraft*. Macmillan.

Mbeki, Thabo. 2004. *Africa Define Yourself*. Cape Town: Tafelberg.

Muchie, Mammo (ed.). 2003. *The Making of Africa-nation: Pan-Africanism and the African Renaissance*. London and Abuja: Adonis and Abbey.

Muchie, Mammo. 2012. 'The Pan-African Roots of the ANC and the African Agenda', (http://www.igd.org.za/jdownloads/IGD%20Reports/anc_sas_foreign_policy_-_proceedings_report.pdf).

Muchie, Mammo, *et al*. (ed.). 2003. *Putting Africa First, The Making of African Innovation Systems*. Aalborg University Press.

Muchie, Matlou and Sasha (eds.). 2011. *The Africana World: From Fragmentation to Unity and Renaissance*. Pretoria: AISA.

Muchie, Phindile and Akpor (eds.). 2013 *The African Union Ten Years After: Solving African Problems with Pan-Africanism and the African-Renaissance*, Pretoria: AISA.

Muchie, Phindile, Vusi and Hailemichael (eds.). 2014. *Unite or Perish: Africa Fifty Years After the Founding of the OAU*. Pretoria: AISA.

https://www.africanunityforrenaissance.wordpress.com/press/

http://www.heritage.org/index/country/southafrica

http://www.kara.co.za/kara-gallery.php?gallery=23#!prettyPhoto[gallery]/

http://www.nesglobal.org/adwa

http://www.nesglobal.org/asapnow/

http://www.thoughtleader.co.za/vusigumede

New African, December, 2014.

New World Wealth: https://www.worldwealthreport.com/

Prah, Kwesi. 2006. *The Africa Nation*. Cape Town: CASAS.

Sabelo J. Ndlovu-Gatsheni. 2014. 'From a "Terrorist" to Global Icon: A Critical Decolonial Ethical Tribute to Nelson Rolihlahla Mandela of South Africa', *Third World Quarterly*, 35(6), July.

Young, Robert Alexander. 1829. *The Ethiopian Manifesto: Issued in Defence of the Blackman's Rights in the Scale of Universal Freedom*. New York.

INNOVATION AND TRANSDISCIPLINARY KNOWLEDGE FOR ACTION – IMRAAN PATEL

I have decided to dispense with a PowerPoint presentation to focus on a set of ideas that may be useful in reflecting on the topic. I will also attempt to apply transdisciplinary thinking in the way that I reflect on the ideas. An important factor in transdisciplinary approaches to knowledge generation is a practitioner's perspective. I have found that academics often talk about transdisciplinarity when they are actually referring to interdisciplinary approaches and the bringing together of various scientific disciplines. Transdisciplinarity is not only about different disciplines coming together, but about mediating and reflecting on different sources of knowledge, whether it's embedded in communities, in business, etc. in order to problem-solve and shape understanding. So, being a practitioner, I would say it's an engagement with the academic community around this. I also want to highlight that, from my understanding, the topic is bringing together two things that in fact require two different engagements. They're quite different, I'll flip between the two, but I could apply a logical framework to both to generate a more coherent analysis. The two issues are that innovation is a bit different to transdisciplinarity from a policy perspective and that the policy imperative for a department of science and technology is how you encourage and support it. So, I'll talk a bit about both, but the emphasis will be on experiences with transdisciplinarity.

The issue here is that the inadequacies of all methods of approaching complex problems are becoming more and more obvious and therefore we require paradigm shifts. I'm not going to argue that we need a paradigm shift. I'm going to take it that there is general agreement at this symposium that we do need a paradigm shift. The focus then moves to two subsidiary questions. The first is: is a paradigm shift possible in South Africa? And the second is: if it's possible, which I would argue it is as there are signals that we are moving in the right direction, how do we accelerate that paradigm shift?

I also want to do what Erika Kraemer-Mbula said: adopt a bit of a systems approach to the issues from the practitioner perspective. So when I look at the paradigm shift, there are a couple of things that are quite important from a funding management perspective. As the Department of Science and Technology, we have access to one of the most significant funding resources that can be used strategically to change behaviour in the system. And part of what we need to think about is how does one do this, if we believe that the science system has to be geared more towards innovation as opposed to just knowledge generation for the sake of knowledge generation. And it needs to do this taking into account that there are new modes of knowledge production; that the kind of wicked problems that we have, whether poverty or inequality or environmental degradation, require us to go beyond boundaries, whether these are disciplinary boundaries or boundaries between different types of knowledge producers.

So funding is a very important enabler of change. I would argue that there are elements where our funding systems in certain ways are trying to facilitate such a change. Four or five years ago, I was responsible for something called the 'Global Change Grand Challenge' and one of the identified interventions was a programme called the 'Global Change Society and Sustainability' research programme. In crafting the programme, we were interested in generating policy-relevant knowledge that would support the sustainability agenda. In working closely with the National Research Foundation (NRF), we realised that the new approach needed to start at the stage of the application form for submitting proposals. So there was a very specific section in the form that required applicants to clearly articulate what is the policy relevance of the research and to provide details on the policy window of opportunity; also: who are the policy stakeholders that you are going to address? We had a process that we went through to evaluate proposals which combined an assessment of the scientific and policy value of the project in a single process. In hindsight, a two-stage process would have worked better: one that included a different way of assessing the policy relevance of the research and the ability for the research to impact on a policy process. We tried to combine it. We had an evaluation committee that included policymakers and the normal kind of peer review processes and I think in some way you need to separate those.

The second example I want to give is a multi-country project funded by Germany called SASSCAL (Southern African Science Service Centre for Climate Change and Adaptive Land Management). When they originally secured funding from the German Government to initiate the project, the concept document said we need to do this in a transdisciplinary way. We need to adopt transdisciplinarity as the basis for this project. I got involved in this project and, if I look at where SASSCAL is now, I would not necessarily say that it's transdisciplinary. And some of the issues related to the fact that you have deep-seated rules and regulations on the side of the German funding and research project management system that mitigated against a truly transdisciplinary effort. In order to effectively report on this funding, the initiative was disaggregated into a set of five research areas of focus. Very little attention was given to creating systems and incentives to find points of intersection and arrangements to bring in alternative knowledge holders. So, there is a mindset around this; there are attempts to change it, but these are not short-term changes, they are deep-seated changes that will require time and an acknowledgement that rules and systems need to be re-purposed. So, that's on the funding systems side.

We also need to think about how we create appropriate institutional arrangements that either place a premium on innovation or place a premium on transdisciplinarity, or both. I would like to give two examples. One is an initiative called Future Earth. This is a major international programme and transdisciplinarity is core to that. They spent more than two or three years thinking through how they do this in an effective way. How do they create the right kinds of incentives; how do they issue calls; how do they even pull together the kind of scientific advisory committee and the steering committees, etc. so that you balance out different sources and holders of knowledge? I think it's a useful case study that requires some reflection at a workshop such as this one. South Africa can benefit from the experiences and techniques for our own system as we are centrally involved through people like Albert van Jaarsveld, who is in the senior leadership, as well as people who are on the Scientific Advisory Committee or the Engagement Committee, etc. Even in that instance, they have recognised that Future Earth will largely focus on the top of the knowledge triangle, where the focus will be on funding support for transdisciplinary efforts built on strong disciplinary strengths supported through national or internal funding arrangements.

Another programme that is more on the innovation side, where there is a focus on issues such as new incentives and new ways of determining what are the research priorities is an initiative called Sector Innovation Funds. Now the important thing about Sector Innovation Funds is that these are intended to find those innovations and technology developments that improve the competitiveness of existing industries. It's important where you place the power around the deployment of the funding. This is done with industry associations. They had to apply to the call and will be managing the priorities and the individual research projects that would be prioritised for funding. Although the bulk of the funding will go to universities and science councils, this creates a very different way of priority setting and enhances the ability of good ideas to be quickly transferred into the real economy. Over the last few years, we had funded two pilot funds that we are now extending. In serving on the steering committee for the sector innovation funds, we realise that there were projects that we thought were important for knowledge generation, but in engaging with industry players it became clear that the knowledge was not likely to make an impact on current challenges being faced by industry. There's also been an added benefit where students are able to be mentored by industry together with an academic supervisor.

Let me quickly list other kinds of issues I would have highlighted had I had time, and maybe there is an opportunity to look at these during the discussion. We need to look at the measurement and monitoring systems used and how these need to change to encourage transdisciplinary research. And I think in some way the measurement framework should have a balanced score card approach or you need to be able to say what are the big issues, like poverty, and then track what is the extent of transdisciplinary research in poverty or in environmental sustainability in addition to looking at what is being done in disciplinary areas.

To end off, we also need to look at what some may call softer factors. Architecture is an important one, where universities are located and based compared to communities, businesses, and other knowledge enterprises. Do you get the BRT systems to stop there? Do you have visitor's centres? Those are very important in terms of crossing disciplinary boundaries. How do you get into schools when you talk about career guidance? How do you give career guidance to someone who wants to adopt a system's view? Does psychometric analysis focus on whether you are good in maths and science, or whether you are able to leverage these strengths in working with people with other strengths, etc.? It's also about creating training programmes. We started a process with universities under the Global Change to talk about a Masters in Earth Systems Science that allows people to combine elements of different sciences.

Time has run out and I have to conclude. I think that South Africa is in a strong position to evolve a very robust innovation system as well as robust systems to advance the practice and application of transdisciplinary research by building on some of the platforms that we have already created. But clearly it is not a short-term journey. Progress will be dependent on progress to deal with a range of lock-ins, including how we think about issues of institutional practices. If I have to think about the next five years, I think we will advance slightly towards this objective.

PART 5

BUILDING A CAPABLE DEVELOPMENTAL STATE

This section explores the developmental state debate in the South African context. The debate, essentially, involves (1) that South Africa is not yet a developmental state and would struggle to become one; (2) that South Africa is a developmental state in the making; and (3) that South Africa is drifting further away from becoming a developmental state. Other important issues include the extent to which the capacity of the post-apartheid state has been developed to address the injustices of the past, to advance human development and foster an inclusive, non-racial and non-sexist society. How does this manifest itself across the spheres of government? What are the achievements and the gaps between expectation and reality on the expressed intention of building a developmental state? And, is the notion of 'developmentalism' shared across the various political schools of thought? Related to this is the expected role of non-state actors in a developmental state.

Building a Capable Developmental State: The State as Enabler and Disruptor – **Parks Tau**

I thought I should preface my input with an indication that, in the multilateral system of governance and the UN systems, local government is generally classified as civil society. Whilst we continue to fight in those forums, I am quite comfortable today to kind of wear the civil society hat. But, just in case I don't succeed with the civil society hat, my profile indicates that I come from the Soweto Youth Congress, the South African Youth Congress and the ANC Youth League, and therefore have the licence that comes with being a youth-leaguer, even though I might have slightly outgrown it.

I suppose I am saying this because, I think the discussion about the developmental state needs to be contrasted with what we have been doing, and we need to ask ourselves the question whether what we have built over the past twenty years has been a developmental state as opposed to a Weberian sort of bureaucratic state that is stuck within the framework of looking at bureaucratic indicators. And think about it: when you look at how government is performing and how we judge government ourselves in the country, in many instances the indicators are what we tend to ask about the performance of departments: what the Standing Committee on Public Accounts (SCOPA) is worried about, the Auditor-General's report, expenditure levels, and all sorts of bureaucratic indicators. And we don't spend enough time, at least in my opinion, evaluating ourselves from the point of view of developmental indicators. So the contrast really, and the question I am asking is, whether, as we debate the notion of a developmental state, there isn't a contrast in there in terms of what we have designed and the output of what we have designed and how we measure ourselves.

Now I am not going to spend time taking us through the background to the evolution of the developmental state: the theoretical framework. I'm sure this would be published so we can make that available to say: look, these are the key characteristics of a developmental state; save to say that a developmental state has a number of critical characteristics. Amongst those is that it is deliberate in its action; it is able to identify specific outputs. Some, in fact, go as far as saying that it is a collusion of the elites – between the political, bureaucratic, business and institutional elites – that tend to meet and have a revolving door that ensures that they are able to deploy resources in a manner that achieves particular outputs.

So there are very many different definitions of the developmental state, but the emphasis is that it does the things that enable us to achieve higher economic growth. It is focused on people. As you bring it closer to home it tends to then be biased in the redistributive elements of what needs to be done. How do we address the injustices of the past? So, not only is its task about the responsibilities going forward, but it also needs to deal with the redistributive elements.

Allow me to say that even the ANC itself has somewhat given a developmental state its own definition, some would argue, adapted to South African conditions ... not to offend those who might feel a bit uncomfortable with a classical definition of the developmental state. And if you go to the NDP itself, I am sitting here with panellists who are members of the Commission; I might get myself into trouble, considering they speak after me, but the reality is that, when the National Planning Commission introduced the concept of what we should do about the state, the emphasis was on its capability and capacity, a tacit acknowledgement that there might be problems in the capacity of the state. And even in the chapter that deals with the developmental state, the emphasis is on a lot of bureaucratic indicators dealing with the capacity, institutional ability and so on and so on, and less emphasis is placed on the development task. Of course, it does have to relate to the objectives of the NDP, but the emphasis in terms of crafting the developmental state, I think, is limited in the way in which it is articulated, largely because we were probably responding to the realities of current-day government challenges that have to do with administration, institutional corruption, spending, and those sorts of things that continue to bedevil government.

And I think that, as we continue to do that, we lose sight sometimes of the nature of the institutions that we have built, which is really the emphasis I would want to place today. And allow me to share an anecdote that actually is not in the paper itself to demonstrate the point. When we, in the City of Johannesburg, were implementing the bus rapid transit (BRT) system there were a number of critical decisions that we made. Amongst those was that the emphasis on ownership should be broad-based. It should emphasise ownership by those who have been providing mass public transport and in this regard the ownership should lie in the hands of the taxi industry, if not as the primary owner, but as the majority owner of the bus rapid transit system.

We also made a decision that the BRT in Johannesburg will start in Soweto. With all the complications that come with implementing a system in Soweto, the battles of the taxi industry and a few deaths away, we were able to implement a bus rapid transit system that is owned by the taxi industry, and currently managed by the taxi industry for that matter. We also made a decision, when we implemented phase 1B of the BRT, we also made a decision to procure buses locally to spur on local growth and development and to incubate industries in bus manufacturing. We began to mobilise our peers and our colleagues, particularly in Gauteng, specifically Tshwane and Ekurhuleni, to collaborate in implementing a programme where we have local bus manufacturers.

But look at how, as a state, we have judged ourselves. The Auditor-General has come back and given us a qualified audit on the basis that we have not capitalised the BRT that is owned by the taxi industry in our books. So if you look at it from an accounting point of view, government is saying: we actually are not impressed with the idea that you have given the people ownership of the BRT, that in fact we are comfortable that you capitalise it in your books because it is designed for the single use of the municipality. So we have to take a number of possible decisions. Either we capitalise it, and of course the industry itself would have to capitalise it because they have their own balance sheets to publish, so they would capitalise it and we would capitalise it in our books so that we meet the indicator that government says, actually, these buses belong to you, notwithstanding the fact that they actually belong to the taxi industry. But that's how we judge ourselves, so we've had to conform and change to now meet the accounting treatment requirements that say, technically, these are our buses, even if they don't belong to us.

Then we go on further and say: well, actually, these buses must be manufactured at a local level; and we made a conscious and deliberate decision that says, even if it means that we would not be able to meet our expenditure targets within the financial year and made the applications to the National Department of Transport that we want to procure the buses locally, this would require a roll-over of the budget into the next financial year because the local industry needs to build up capacity to meet our requirements. The reality is that we were unable to spend the money in the financial year where the money was allocated. The judgment ultimately was under-expenditure by the City of Johannesburg on the BRT. And at no point did anybody say: there is a rider to your annual financial statement that says that you are procuring these buses locally so that you can create local jobs.

So the argument, at least from my point of view, is that what we have tended to do is rather measure ourselves against administrative and bureaucratic indicators, and place less emphasis on the development objectives and indicators. And how we judge ourselves, and how the instruments of review judge us, is based on those indicators. Therefore, I would argue that there are a number of critical things that we need to do in terms of how we redesign our legislative, financial, fiscal and other instruments and mechanisms of moral suasion to enable the state to be more developmental so that we begin judging the state from a development point of view as opposed to judging it simply from a bureaucratic point of view. This is not because we shouldn't worry about expenditure, about accountability and, and, and … we should worry about those things, but the task is much bigger than those things and we should have legislation that enables, as opposed to stifles, the ability.

I can go on with many examples. It is easier to build houses for the poor in the periphery, in the middle of nowhere, and reinforce apartheid spatial patterns than it is to confront the reality of our morphology as apartheid cities and apartheid-designed cities that exclude poor Black people from the urban amenities and locks them into dormitory townships. So our history in the past twenty years has been to build RDP houses in the middle of nowhere, and I'm sure Verwoerd doesn't think that we are doing particularly badly in terms of reinforcing what his ideas were; but our subsidies are designed for that so that's how the system works.

Now, I've got in the paper itself a few examples of what we could and should do to drive a developmental state, but because I've run out of time I won't go through them, save to share one that I think is critical, partly because I am a local government practitioner. I am an urban practitioner from the point of view of having been in the City of Johannesburg for … I've even forgotten the duration … I was City Manager, that's how long I have been in the system. So confronting the reality of the apartheid city has to do with confronting its morphology, its structure, its system, how it works, and for you to be able to do that you need to build a different city that integrates people into the city that does a number of things, and I'll just make two examples and then nothing more.

The first is: is our transport subsidy system designed to enable those who live in the peripheral margins of our city to access the city? Our transport subsidy system is designed like any classical transport subsidy system that says: the further away you live, the more you pay. In fact, we do not want to incentivise you to live far away from town, but the reality is that we've designed and located the people far away from town, so we continue to marginalise them in the way in which we subsidise the buses themselves. So we could actually change the subsidy system to acknowledge that the poor live in the periphery and therefore we need to give them greater access into the city through mobility and through reliable public transport. Something that we'd have to consider, as opposed to conforming to standard practices that say the further you are the more we disincentivise how you access the city, because the reality is that it is not voluntary suburbanisation, it is because our cities are designed as such.

The second relates to building a city that enables greater access from the point of view of where the houses and opportunities are, in terms of proximity and accessibility to facilities. The reality is, if you look at our current housing subsidy systems, if you look at our current town planning systems, including the recently promulgated Spatial and Land Use Management Act, they do not incentivise or enable municipalities to make the decisions that say: we will build the houses in a manner that integrates our cities. They continue to literally force us into an environment where we have to put the people in the periphery, and you have to take some difficult decisions from a practitioner's point of view to begin to navigate that, and whilst we are attempting to navigate it, the reality is that we are in unchartered territories.

We have published in Johannesburg what we call the 'Corridors of Freedom', which are high-intensity, high-density integrated land use corridors in the core of the City of Johannesburg. The policy has just been adopted, but I can tell you that the instruments that are at our disposal are not necessarily enabling, so we are going to navigate a very difficult and arduous process of building opportunities for people closer to the city; but the reality is, unless we do that and unless we begin forcing legislation to answer these questions, then we are not going to resolve the problems.

Formal Paper Prepared in Support of Verbal Presentation – Parks Tau

Abstract

The concept of a developmental state, a term originally coined to describe the purpose-built state-led economic machine that was post WWII Japan, is now applied with a crucial customisation across continental Africa, and in southern Africa in particular. The developmental state must not just lead the full scope of social forces to realise economic growth, but must also directly confront and redress the inequalities and social imbalances bequeathed by our colonial past. It is crucial to interrogate whether we are indeed putting in place such a purpose-driven, coherent state machine. As it stands, my answer to such an interrogation is that we are not – we are, instead, increasingly structuring and measuring ourselves as a bureaucratic state. To transition to a capable developmental state requires a range of radical measures that would put the state at the heart of the transformational process, most notably in a leadership role.

CONCEPTUAL FRAMEWORK

Theories of the Developmental State

If we work from the early 80s version of the developmental state, developed by Chalmers Johnson to describe a rising post-WWII Japan and then appropriated to describe the rise of the Asian Tigers and the rapid development of Latin America in the early 2000s, we can describe the developmental state or 'hard' state as a purposeful instrument enabling a specific set of macro-economic goals, cohering the various levers of state to achieve them (particularly in the more recent theories of Chang and Cummings). While not exhaustive, it provides a starting block on which to cut and shape a useful definition of the developmental state for the purposes of this discussion.

South African Definition and Customisation

In the early to mid-2000s, a range of useful thinking emerged, interpreting the developmental state in a southern African context (see, for example, Ikpe, 2008). The major distinguishing features re-purpose the developmental state, not to respond purely to the goal of GDP growth and macroeconomic development, but specifically to remedying the imbalances wrought by the colonial and apartheid eras. This gives the developmental state a redistributive agenda, or, at the very least, a much more pronounced emphasis on uplifting the economically dispossessed and socially deprived.

The ANC, as the governing party, has enhanced this definition through the various iterations of the Strategy and Tactics document, assigning the state an aggressive and critical leadership role in realising the aspiration of the national democratic society – one that is truly non-racial, non-sexist, and prosperous.

Problematising the Developmental State

The question posed by the working Southern African definition is thus two-fold: firstly, how can the state machinery be harnessed to a specific set of macro-economic goals (and be equipped to mobilise and influence other non–state actors to follow suit), and secondly, what does such a process look like when the economic goal in question is combining economic growth with increasing equity?

Have we worked towards 'a state' machinery that can lead the wider social forces to realise these complex transformational goals, or are we constructing something quite different, which answers to different masters?

Developmental vs Bureaucratic Design

In assessing what kind of state we are in the process of building over the last two decades, we must recognise that most state administrations remain hostages of Max Weber. The professional bureaucracy that emerged in the mid-nineteenth century on the European continent was idealised by Weber as a critical platform for the management of modern public affairs. It places emphasis – in designing organisational forms – on tightly structured hierarchy to drive decision-making, clear lines of procedural controls and prudent stewardship of state resources.

I suspect that is a definition the Auditor-General would still find quite pleasing.

It honours important principles such as accountability and transparency, and can do much to promote efficiency when it comes to well understood and predictable public tasks like collecting garbage every Monday. But it is a poor platform for innovation – and innovation is precisely what is required when taking on the complex transformational tasks we have assigned to the developmental state.

We should clarify that this analysis by no means suggests that the developmental state should tolerate inefficiency or lack of accountability – quite the opposite. In this sense, the bureaucratic state is not the antithesis of the developmental state. There is no reason, for a start, that both models cannot place an emphasis on strong, results-driven management and clear organisational accountability. But the emphasis and architecture of principles in the models is different enough to have profound consequences.

To the extent that we are transparent, accountable, well organised and prudent – by King III or any other measure – we have met the highest standards of the bureaucratic state. But the developmental state requires us to go much further, often into unchartered territory for the public sector. It requires a different kind of state organisation and a different kind of state practitioner.

We can start by considering more precisely what we need this new kind of state organisation to do.

The Mission of the Developmental State

A useful place in our public discourse to begin when setting out what a capable developmental state should look like is with the NDP chapter, which addresses precisely that question.

Limitations of the NDP conceptualisation and definition:

The National Development Plan 2030 dedicates a full chapter to building a capable developmental state, but focuses narrowly on questions of capacity, professional bureaucracy and administrative efficiency. While useful, this does not cut to the heart of specifying how the developmental state should be organised and operate. The developmental state by definition cannot be goal-agnostic. The nine areas of defined intervention laid out by the NDP provide specific content to the goals of the state but need further interrogation, specifically in terms of what a capable developmental state would do to realise these goals. It is a fair description of what we expect from a bureaucratic state.

Later on in this paper, we address that more directly with respect to education and skills, political economy of space, and energy mix. But before we do so, we must frame all of these within the broader developmental goal we assign to the state machinery.

The political calibration of the developmental state:

We must be clear in our minds that, unlike the bureaucratic state, the developmental state is not a politically neutral institution. As Australian political scientist, John Wanna, noted in his influential 2010 work on active policy making:[1]

> *Every stage of the policy process is political (the design phase, the action phase, and the review phase) ... By definition ... policy is inherently political because governments are attempting to change circumstances that would otherwise prevail. Policy has a political purpose: it is aimed to effect outcomes in politically sanctioned directions.*

The capable developmental state must recognise and harness the productive impact of such a driving tension, building political calibration into its operations and making it the animating spirit with which it directs the symphony of resources and interest groups in the realisation of defined goals.

Wanna goes on to point out that:

> *Politics is not solely about decisive capacity or administrative capability but also about building relationships within and between institutions and organisations, with communities of interest and even between individuals ... Policy-making does not stop when implementation starts.*[2]

To be capable, the developmental state must recognise this dynamic and empower itself to be effective at such relationship building.

THE DEVELOPMENTAL IMPERATIVE

A Theoretical Framework for Intervention: the Developmental State as Disruptor and Enabler

In his book, *Development as Freedom,* the Nobel prize-winning economist Amartya Sen defines development as 'enlarging people's choices, capabilities and freedoms, so that they can live a long and healthy life, have access to knowledge, a decent standard of living, and participate in the life of their community'.

As Barder has summarised the Sen position: 'Development should be judged not only on the basis of increases in average incomes, but on whether it creates the circumstances for people ... to exercise their choices, capabilities and freedoms.'

To drive development that meets this wider set of objectives, we must deepen our understanding of how to intervene productively in the political economies the state seeks to influence, and in so doing re-engineer distribution, taking into account the balance of forces from time to time.

The base document of the thirteenth Johannesburg Regional ANC conference provides us with a clear theoretical framework for how the state can act as a disruptor of closed, unequal markets and an accelerator for radical socio-economic transformation.

As Thabo Mbeki declared to the world in his famed speech on historical injustice in Ottawa, Canada in 1978:

> *We must, by liberating ourselves, make our own history. Such a process by its nature imposes on the activist the necessity to plan and therefore requires the ability to measure cause and effect; the necessity to strike in correct directions and hence the requirement to distinguish between essence and phenomenon; the necessity to move millions of people as one man to actual victory and consequently the development of the skill of combining the necessary and the possible.*

The injustice Mbeki was then urging the liberation movement and the world at large to mobilise against began, as he detailed in said speech, with the economic disenfranchisement of the many. He drew, as many of us do, on the piercing Marxist argument that how the economics of a society is organised determines how the social structure of that society works – known ever since as the *base-superstructure* argument.[3] The economic base determines the social super-structure.

Furthermore, as the economist Thomas Piketty has argued so convincingly in his recent book, *Capital in the Twenty-First Century*,[4] inequality has proved persistent and deepening precisely because the returns to capital (ownership or equity value in the means of production) historically and increasingly exceed the returns to labour. In other words, those who own pieces of firms that serve a growing economy or have cash reserves to invest will earn consistently more than those who are merely employees, however high and far those employees strive. This presents a challenge to the widely influential proclamations of economists such as Simon Kuznetz (the thinker behind the famous u-curve describing the relationship between development, employment levels and inequality) in the 1950's that, over time, returns to capital and labour will be equal – an assumption which has been used to justify a lack of state action to correct this deepening inequality.

Wider participation in the economy at the value-sharing level is critical in ensuring that a rising tide does indeed raise all boats, as Kuznetz and his followers have always believed. We believe that radical change in the economic basis of society must be achieved by removing barriers to entry for all classes, races and genders – particularly the poor, and deconcentrating economic activity in ways compatible with the trade relations – person to person, firm to firm – that is the lifeblood of everyday prosperity flowing from the earliest civilisations.

Being radical in a progressive context is not about dogmatic adherence to established notions, however long-held those notions may be. Being radical is by nature disruptive, but also pragmatic. In the context of the massive socio-economic changes we must enable to fulfil the transformative promises of our governing mandate, 'being radical' should mean aggressively departing from the status quo to enable and, where necessary, force rapid, sustainable and meaningful change to the conditions on the ground and the socio-economic realities and systems that have produced these conditions.

It means recognising that we must liberate our people to be economic agents, using those powers available to the developmental state – and those it might acquire through appropriate motivation and policy change – to engineer shifts in the balances of forces driving the economy, social conditions and the capabilities of the state itself. In enabling change in the base, in transforming the enabling conditions of economic life – promoting access to markets, access to space, access to the city – we will enable the changes in the social superstructure we so desperately need to see.

This approach follows strong conceptual paths cut by some of the most influential developmental economy thought leaders of our time. Hernando De Soto[5] has long demonstrated through his work that economic title and formal economic participation by those who currently trade and live informally are the bedrock conditions of widespread economic upliftment. C. K. Pralahad famously urged business and governments globally to seek the 'fortune at the bottom of the pyramid' by empowering the poor as economic agents – as both consumers and producers.[6]

This also dovetails with critical insights promoted by the noted champion of urban diversity and the liberation potential of cities, David Harvey, who advises us that one way to unify our ideological and practical positions is:

> to focus on the right to the city as both a working slogan and a political ideal, precisely because it focuses on who it is that commands the inner connection that has prevailed from time immemorial between urbanization and surplus production and use. The democratization of the right to the City and the construction of a broad social movement to enforce its will is imperative, if the dispossessed are to take back control of the city from which they have so long been excluded and if new modes of controlling capital surpluses as they work through urbanization processes are to be instituted … the revolution has to be urban, in the broadest sense of that term, or nothing at all.

The state must continue to mobilise society in its broadest sense to participate in both the process of governing and development in order to realise a more equitable city.

In this paradigm, the key tasks that face the state going forward entail continuing to pursue policies that seek to transform apartheid relations of production, with emphasis on bettering the lives of the poor and the vulnerable. To accelerate local action for radical socio-economic transformation requires intervention to fundamentally transform the economy, society and the state. What follows presents more detailed proposals to this effect.

Flowing from the NDP, we can look at three specific examples of how the state can disrupt conditions that hamper development and enable conditions that accelerate it.

Disruptor/ Enabler 1: Political Economy of Space

Our towns and our major cities alike remain museums of apartheid spatial morphology. Johannesburg, for example, remains the largest metropolitan centre, and continues to attract migrants (both national and cross-border). Notwithstanding the difficulties associated with accurately predicting the number of foreign migrants in the city, Johannesburg has become increasingly diverse and cosmopolitan.

Certainly one of the most striking statistics to emerge from the 2011 census shows the migration effect from other provinces into Gauteng in general and Johannesburg in particular. The migration figures from Census 2011 demonstrate that Gauteng as a province has received 568,000 net migrants in the period from 2007 to 2011. This arguably represents a flight to economic opportunity, but it is also clear that the flight of low-skill-working age individuals from other provinces will add to the populations accommodating themselves informally at the urban periphery.[7]

With respect to the political economy of space, mobility determines access to the city. How much it costs you to access economic activity is a major determinant of where you can afford to live, and is the lock-out factor for those seeking to be active in the city's economy without significant means at their disposal. Particularly those located at the periphery incur transport costs equivalent to 25 to 30 per cent of their monthly expenditure (with indications that this percentage may be as high as 40 per cent for certain groups). Gauteng Household Survey data shows these costs are highest as a percentage of people's budgets for households within incomes between R400 (those earning below can afford only limited transport and therefore spend relatively less) and R10,000 per month, who will struggle to access the urban core as residents of better located areas on account of the costs of housing.

The 'Corridors of Freedom Programme' is the leading edge of an approach that must ultimately alter the spatial destiny of the city. Left to the forces of the market alone, the poor would be cast to the edges of the city, renting shacks on the informal market, huddled together in high-density settlements far outstripping the carrying capacity of the utilities installed to serve them, and trapped by the mobility cost conundrum just discussed. These settlements would be found far from the wealthy living a low-density existence on high-value property in highly developed, urban zones with the working and middle classes trapped in entry-level rentals and gated communities at the urban edge, reliant on traffic-choked roads to access economic opportunity. To an unfortunate extent, this is the emerging Jo'burg reality. To undo this reality requires reshaping the use of space by government (with respect to public transportation, public environment and the use of state property) and the incentives governing how space is used by the private sector. That demonstrates the combination of direct action and social compact required to realise developmental goals – and is, in point of fact, a microcosm of the spatial challenge at the national level. The state must combine the levers it directly controls – programmes, legislation, taxation, and fiscal incentives – with the moral suasion required to bring non-state actors onside with stated developmental goals.

DISRUPTOR/ENABLER 2: FROM ENERGY MIX TO AN ENERGY STRATEGY

Energy supply and cost consistently rank amongst the most cited challenges in both the areas of fostering new business and raising standards of living. Regulators, pundits and commentators alike rally around the concept of an energy mix, which – depending on whom you ask and in which context – includes coal, nuclear and renewables.

Pockets of innovation – such as coal to liquid fuel conversion – are isolated successes and do not constitute an energy strategy clearly harnessed to wider – and more equitable – economic development objectives. The market suffers from a collective action problem: it is not worth any one provider's while to invest in the platforms and systems which make new forms of energy available to consumers. The state must choose which forms of energy it shepherds to market via regulation and incentives, and where necessary must build the distribution systems. Where the state does not lead with enabling infrastructure the market will not follow.

What kind of market dynamics we seek to enable should take far more account of our strategic endowments and balance these against the imperatives of moving towards a low-carbon economy. Most critically, our energy policy must, in fact, be an energy strategy, drawing on areas of economic strength to create vast, new and widespread opportunities – for example, drawing on our extensive platinum supply to build out the next generation of hydrogen fuel cells. That requires an extensive coordination effort by the state, once again forming a social compact with the market.

Disruptor/ Enabler 3: Education/Skills

A Mismatch Between the Academy and the Economy

The World Bank Development Report on Jobs 2013 carries an explicit warning to those who place blind faith in educational/skills participation (the supply side of the labour force) without paying at least equal attention to the demand profile for skills in the economy itself. The result, as with Tunisia before the Arab Spring, is that countries can find themselves in a position of reasonably strong economic growth and high levels of university graduation and yet experience stubborn levels of graduate unemployment. In Tunisia's case, this was due to cronyism in a public sector dominated workforce that locked far too many graduates out. It is worth remembering that the young man who sparked the protests which began the Arab Spring was an unemployed graduate who had just had the fruit he was selling to survive confiscated by corrupt officials – in a year when Tunisia recorded five per cent economic growth and high levels of university enrolment. This is by way of reminding ourselves that education, while critical, needs to operate in full consciousness of its economic context. Here at home, we have a similar contextual failure in that education systems are only partially serving as a preparatory phase of the workforce development system.

This ties in with a critical argument made by Thomas Piketty – mainstream economic theory argues that the diffusion of education and skills is a major force pushing convergence between returns to labour and returns to capital – in other words, it is through education and skills development that those who cannot rely on inherited wealth raise their incomes and hence their standard of living. Piketty argues that this is not a sufficient counterweight to the advantages of being an owner of capital, since returns to capital over time are higher than returns to labour. **Education is a necessary but not sufficient condition for addressing historical burdens as the economy strives for sustainable growth and development.**

The state here is clearly best placed to disrupt the existing market through which all levels of education are provided and take the lead in evolving the newer, better systems that should replace it. **This often means coordinating between the education system, the labour market, society at large and the wider economy, harnessing state institutions to a common coordinated strategy.**

This requires transforming the system along a continuum – starting at its present state and advancing to the point where the private sector, the SETAs and educational establishments operate under a common workforce development strategy linked to specific economic goals.

These goals should be those that make the most feasible and productive use of our natural endowments and strategic advantages as an economy.

We must leapfrog to new forms of economic opportunity but, in order for us to leapfrog, these various forces need to act in a coordinated manner, and the state must lead them.

The state must be the coordinator and leader of such a process to ensure that both inclusivity and equity are at the heart of the endeavour. This is one subset of the social compact the state must facilitate.

Conclusion

The state cannot claim to be developmental and not make specific and far-reaching choices on the nature of the transformation it seeks to effect. Our argument here is that the state must act as both disruptor of dysfunctional (often oligopolistic) markets and modes of provision, and an enabler of the socio-economic realities it seeks to bring into being. This cannot be done through direct action alone. The capable developmental state must lead as well as act, forging a social compact with the relevant parties and complementing such partnerships with its own actions in the form of strategically deployed regulation, incentives, fiscal policies and programmes. If we fail at these two very non-traditional roles of the state, South Africa will indeed drift further and further away from becoming a truly capable developmental state.

End Notes

1. Wanna, J., *et al.* 2010. *Policy in Action: The Challenge of Service Delivery*. New South Wales: University of New South Wales Press.
2. op. cit.
3. Marx explains the Base-Superstructure Model as follows in his preface to *A Contribution to the Critique of Political Economy* (1859):
   'In the social production of their existence, men inevitably enter into definite relations, which are independent of their will, namely [the] relations of production appropriate to a given stage in the development of their material forces of production. The totality of these relations of production constitutes the economic structure of society, the real foundation, on which arises a legal and political superstructure, and to which correspond definite forms of consciousness. The mode of production of material life

conditions the general process of social, political, and intellectual life. It is not the consciousness of men that determines their existence, but their social existence that determines their consciousness. At a certain stage of development, the material productive forces of society come into conflict with the existing relations of production, or — this merely expresses the same thing in legal terms — with the property relations within the framework of which they have operated hitherto. From forms of development of the productive forces, these relations turn into their fetters. Then begins an era of social revolution. The changes in the economic foundation lead, sooner or later, to the transformation of the whole immense superstructure. In studying such transformations, it is always necessary to distinguish between the material transformation of the economic conditions of production, which can be determined with the precision of natural science, and the legal, political, religious, artistic, or philosophic — in short, ideological forms in which men become conscious of this conflict and fight it out. Just as one does not judge an individual by what he thinks about himself, so one cannot judge such a period of transformation by its consciousness, but, on the contrary, this consciousness must be explained from the contradictions of material life, from the conflict existing between the social forces of production and the relations of production.'

4. Piketty, T. 2014. *Capital in the 21st Century*. Arthur Goldhammer (Trans.), Cambridge, MA: Belknap Press of Harvard University Press.

5. De Soto, H. 2000. *The Mystery of Capital: Why Capitalism Triumphs in the West and Fails Everywhere Else*. London: Bantam.

6. Pralahad, C. K. 2006. *The Fortune at the Bottom of the Pyramid*. Upper Saddle River, NJ: Pearson Education Ltd.

7. Cross-border migrant flows are far more complex to track given the percentage of irregularity. The African Centre for Migration and Society (ACMS) estimated in its 2010 fact sheet that cross-border migrants constituted 1.6–2 million of the total national population (3–4%) (Polzer, 2010). That being said, there is significant instability and circularity, as demonstrated even by regular channels. For example, in 2009, 223,324 asylum seekers applied nationally, 4,567 were approved, 46,055 were rejected and 172,702 were added to the backlog of unprocessed cases. Over the two years previous (2007–08), 312,733 were deported (ibid.).

The trend analysis here would therefore suggest that internal migrant flows will account for approximately 10 times the level of cross-border migrant flows into the city.

BUILDING A CAPABLE DEVELOPMENTAL STATE – **RAENETTE TALJAARD**

I am very pleased that I was introduced as Ms and not as Commissioner because I don't want my title as a Commissioner to inhibit my candour on the topic. So I will let out my inner academic and I will hopefully be provocative and controversial in some of the issues I want to place before you. Before I address the issues of the capable developmental state debate, I want to make a bold assertion that, despite the transition to democracy and the transformation efforts that have been made and the plethora of legislative changes that have been made, there are core elements of the state that have not significantly broken away from the deeper embedded institutional culture of the apartheid state, or where elements of these traits remain latent, and I am making this argument deliberately because I wish to return to it.

In this regard, I want to invoke what happened recently with the Marikana massacre for a very deliberative reason, because for me Marikana surely speaks to something much deeper, to an embedded institutional culture that rests deep within the South African state that shows traces of the past in the present and that hamstrings the state's efforts to think through developmental paradigms of a consultative nature more carefully. I know this is provocative and it is intended to be so. This is a bold assertion which would require an entire panel discussion of its own, so what I will try to do is to stick to the knitting of what I was given to do, which is to look at the developmental state. But I do believe that what we are looking at, particularly if we look at the experience of the Marikana massacre, are institutional embedded cultures that have not necessarily transcended and moved deeper into where we want our country to be in a consultative developmental paradigm. But what is this developmental state? And I'll take my lead from Mayor Tau and not go into the characteristics themselves.

But what I do wish to do is just to hint on some of the origins, clearly from East Asia, as well as in our own region – Botswana is often invoked as an example of a developmental state – and if we look at the discourses on beneficiation it's certainly an interesting and compelling argument. In addition, Japan and the role of the Ministry of International Trade and Industry is often invoked as a core example. I'll rest with those examples and simply state that it's clear that South Africa's National Development Plan is infused with notions of a capable developmental state, and as such the assumption, therefore, is that it is a clear and desirable goal of the South African state.

In addition, and perhaps ironically, the 'good governance' debate, given where its origins lie, is intimately wrapped up in the discourse about a capable developmental state, despite the baggage that the concept carries and has carried, if one looks at the works of Merilee Grindle of Harvard, and her most recent works on 'good enough governance' and 'good enough governance revisited'. Equally ironically, the much and rightly criticised World Bank has produced a series, quite a fascinating series, called *The Capable State Series* which has looked at the role of the state in engineering enterprises in Korea, Chile, Tanzania, India and Uganda; the role of the state in better caring for its most vulnerable citizens: the elderly, unemployed and homeless in Russia, China, Senegal and India; and the role of anti-corruption programmes that aim at fostering more open, transparent governments and promoting greater citizens' participation in decision-making in Uganda, Singapore and Brazil. And from the content of these specific programmes, you can already hear that you are dealing with a different intonation of what a capable developmental state could look like and how it interacts with the citizenry and the more active citizenry.

So how does South Africa's capable developmental state stack up against this list of characteristics of a developmental state, and what are some of the areas for focus of the ever-present, though controversial, good governance or good enough governance discourse on this particular debate? Firstly, it's uncontroversial: we have a mixed economy. Secondly, what is clearly more controversial: we have elements of dysfunction in our social compact structures and in our social dialogue institutions, specifically Nedlac's inability to live up to its legislative intent and the divided union and labour constituencies that are now matching up a divided business constituency. Thirdly, there are elements of dysfunction in our state-owned entities, and these are entities that can be expected to play a much greater role in the developmental state; but there are elements of dysfunction in our state-owned entities and regulatory bodies, despite considerable sunken investment with respect to the Presidential Review Panel on SOEs, and some of its findings on reform. Fourthly, our bureaucracy is arguably hallmarked by high turnover rates tied to (and here is a controversy once more), amongst other factors, succession battles in parties that spill over into state structures.

This arguably plagues all political parties in government at different levels of government – please note, all political parties in government at different levels of government. Fifthly, during the early years of democracy, South Africa had a necessary focus on political reform and building institutions and, in my view, an insufficient focus on economic reform of a deep and profound structural kind beyond the real and exigent pressures of global capital, bearing in mind it was the end of the Cold War era and expectations of the dominance of a particular model.

In keeping with the themes of this panel, my contention therefore will be, and is, that South Africa is not yet a developmental state and indeed would struggle to become one, and furthermore, arguably, that South Africa is drifting further away from becoming a developmental state. This is a dialogue – and I am being provocative – that must be furthered and focused if we are going to grapple with the evolving challenges that we face. Worse still, if you look at the juxtapositions that are made, you have a developmental state that is set in juxtaposition with either a weak or a predatory state. That is what the literature suggests on the topic. Whilst the correct growth constraints have been identified and are the target of significant quantities of public expenditure, investments in human capital, in education and health, and indeed in addressing infrastructure constraints of a physical nature, there are significant challenges ahead to ensure a greater focus on sustainable and equitable societal change.

In keeping with the approach followed by yesterday's presentation by the Deputy Chief Justice, I'd like to identify at least four areas of focus that I believe can contribute to sustained change and transformation if they are specifically addressed and given sufficient in-depth attention. I know they do not lie in the arena of macro-economic policy for those of you who may have believed that they do. Forgive me if they sound less economically focused, but I believe they also constitute sites of current contestation that are impacting on the capability of the state, whether developmental or otherwise.

The first: trust in public institutions. If we look at successive Human Sciences Research Council (HSRC) surveys, we can clearly see that there is a crisis in trust in public institutions. This has an impact with respect to inter-generational views of ownership over the institutions of state, and it is an issue that I've certainly had a lot of exposure to this year in my other role when I was listening to focus groups of born-free young South Africans leading into this electoral cycle. So trust in public institutions and an inter-generational view of ownership because if, inter-generationally, there is not a sense of ownership over institutions (there can be a discourse on the nature of the state), if there is no sense of ownership, the state will be engaged in a confrontational stance with younger generations of South Africans.

Secondly, corruption as a fundamentally eroding factor – and in this regard I must say that this is an area that compromises and could compromise the very essence of the fabric of the state and compromise its role whether developmental or otherwise. Again, here the role and standard that were recently set by the Constitutional Court in the Allpay case and the Sassa tender set a new standard in terms of Section 217 of our Constitution, which is of critical importance if we are going to pursue an ethically-founded developmental state.

Thirdly, we are confronting, as the macro-economic reality, profound fiscal breaks and constraints. We are running twin deficits. We are at a debt-to-GDP ratio that looks very similar to the advent of our democracy when the debt-to-GDP ratio was at a similar level. So there are fiscal breaks and constraints that are becoming quite profound.

Fourthly, and here I perhaps stray into a different arena where I do have a different institutional role, I would suggest to you that there is a crucial and critical role to be played by Chapter 9 constitutional institutions. These entities are force multipliers for the legislature and for the executive potentially. That is the way the Constitution set them up and that is the way in which they ought to be functioning if we are going to have, once again, a properly functioning developmental capable state. Pregs Govender spoke yesterday about the work that the Human Rights Commission has done focusing on water and sanitation. That work of the South African Human Rights Commission was profoundly important, and not necessarily well received, either within the legislative or executive space, but profoundly important if you are looking at debates about a developmental state trying to grapple with whether the right policy decisions were made with cost recovery on the commodification of water. These are very profound questions to be asking, and it is right and just that a Chapter 9 constitutional institution such as the Human Rights Commission asks these questions. So I would suggest to you that the role of Chapter 9s as force multipliers for the executive and the legislature in pursuing a developmental agenda is non-negotiable and critical.

The Deputy Chief Justice's focus on land reform inequality also led me to think of the work of Thomas Piketty in his book *Capital in the Twenty-First*

Century, which focuses on the distribution of capital and the incidence of inequality, and I just want to quote from Piketty's recent publication. The second conclusion, which is at the heart of the book, is that the dynamics of wealth distribution reveal powerful mechanisms pushing alternately towards convergence and divergence. Furthermore, there is no natural spontaneous process to prevent destabilising inegalitarian forces from prevailing permanently. Piketty's work is raising profound and uncomfortable questions about the distribution of capital and the incidence of inequality, which calls out for debate and discussion in the South African contemporary context.

These questions arise, and they obviously arise in a loaded context due to the dynamics of our history despite twenty years of democracy. However, if one considers the powerful insights also shared yesterday by Mazibuko K. Jara, it's quite important to flesh out what he said, and I actually wrote down word for word what he said because of its provocative nature in the context of Piketty's work. How do we move to a firm dialogue that focuses on the poor? We are very far away from that. This is the perspective from the Left. But there is clearly increasingly a mainstream awareness that this is a reality of where the contemporary South African discourse is twenty years after democracy. How we find the modalities for that dialogue, how we find the requisite levels of honesty to have that dialogue, is where the challenge really lies in substantive terms.

Over the years, there have been numerous demands for an economic Codesa. Economic policy cannot be negotiated in quite the same legal, technical form that constitutions can be, and I'm not saying that that was either an easy or only a technical process. There are limitations to the analogies of the Codesa that led to the Constitution and an economic Codesa. It's perhaps worth consideration, and perhaps MISTRA can take the lead here to host a series of highly focused Piketty-inspired lectures on the crisp questions of capital distribution and inequality through the lens of some of the challenging analytical issues highlighted yesterday by the Deputy Chief Justice.

As a public policy scholar, I will conclude in my last minute with perhaps the most controversial provocative thought I wish to raise, particularly given the forum in which we are. I'd like to just share the concern, which is not often spoken about as openly, that the challenge is perhaps mildly unique in South Africa in our effort to bring substantive and long-term sustainable societal change in an environment where we are often gripped by a near constant succession dynamic which is inimical to policy focus, and equally inimical to substantive long-term change. They are certainly diametrically opposed to the building of a capable developmental state, and may in truth and in fact be part and parcel of paving the way for a more predatory or weak state that may even show signs of the deeper institutional culture of the past state, as opposed to being infused by the founding values in the preamble to the Constitution. It is our collective duty to work for the constitutional vision of a state infused by human development imperatives, as our Bill of Rights makes clear with respect to progressive realisation to which other giants in the room have contributed enormously through their jurisprudence.

BUILDING A CAPABLE AND DEVELOPMENTAL STATE – PASCAL MOLOI

THE NATION

It is appropriate to describe South Africa as a nation state even before we explore whether it is developmental or not. I came across this definition, which I found useful: 'a nation state is a geographical area that can be identified as deriving its political legitimacy from serving as a sovereign nation. A state is a political and geopolitical entity, while a nation is a cultural and ethnic one. The term "nation state" implies that the two coincide, but "nation state" formation can take place at different times in different parts of the world, and has become the dominant form of world organization.'

The nation state in South Africa was formally instituted with the 1994 election and the inauguration of Nelson Mandela as its first president. Since then, this multicultural and many ethnicities nation has been hard at work to build a political system and entities that would cement its identity as a nation located at the southern-most tip of the continent with a common history of subjugation and struggle. It built a constitution with defined rights, obligations and responsibilities. It adopted common symbols to define itself such as the flag, the springbok and the protea. It built on common phrases and slang that are now recognisable as purely South African such as *lekker*, *lapa* (taken from the seSotho word *lelapa* referring to a thatched roof structure), *Amaglug-glug*, *Banyana-Banyana*, 'sufficient consensus' (popularised during the early 90s negotiations), and *ubuntu*. It is the international home of the *vuvuzela*.

That South Africa is not yet a developmental state and would struggle to become one?

It is difficult, noting where we come from, not to recognise the progress we have made as a state over the last two decades. Development is a continuous process and over the years we have embarked on projects that in themselves are developmental. These include:

- going through and managing the process of finding the truth about our history of conflict and finding reconciliation through the Truth and Reconciliation Commission;
- building a government of national unity and adopting a constitution;
- forming parliament, government and the judiciary;
- building a variety of platforms to allow various communities to find each other such as Nedlac, The National Peace Accord and the Anti-Corruption Forum;
- establishing institutions to defend our democracy and the right to be heard such as the Electoral Commission, the Office of the Public Protector and other Chapter 9 Institutions; and
- developing and experimenting with a number of government policies aimed at redressing apartheid spatial segregation, extending access to basic services, health and education.

It's easy to conclude that we are and have been a state under reconstruction and development.

The National Development Plan concentrates in its Chapter 13 on the notion of a developmental and capable state. It does so to recognise that, for the state to be truly developmental, the political system and its mechanisms have to be capable. It produced a diagnosis that concluded that a capable state is a critical requirement to achieve our developmental aspirations as a nation.

The capability of the state, including parliament, government (and its spheres and agencies) and the judiciary, is necessary:

- to build the economy with strong requisite infrastructure;
- to protect our limited resources and environment;
- to build social cohesion;
- to encourage and allow citizens and communities to be active players in their own development; and
- to build sustainable and dignified human settlements that are safe with a decent standard of living defined by access to water, sanitation, energy, roads, health, education and transportation.

To achieve these, the state has to be led, run and managed by men and women who are capable, competent and driven by the desire to serve the public. They have to be able to build institutions that are strong, reliable and sustainable. Institutions are only as good as the processes, systems and people they employ and their relevance towards meeting the needs of the nation and particularly the poor.

That South Africa is drifting further away from becoming a developmental state?

There are definite signs that if we do not sustain and build on what we began with over the last twenty years, our trajectory towards meeting our developmental objectives may be stalled, derailed or even halted.

Building a capable and developmental state is one of the six pillars that support the National Development Plan. There are indeed worrying trends that suggest serious challenges in sustaining these pillars.

- Mobilisation of all South Africans: our success rests on all South Africans being mobilised to appreciate our development path and support it. While there has been a lot of talk and engagement on the Plan, the extent to which the state can claim to have mobilised sufficient support is yet to be tested.
- Active engagement of citizens in their own development: the state cannot achieve the implementation of the Development Plan alone. Citizens and their representative bodies should be engaged as development partners. The state at different levels and sectors has to enter into a solid social contract with civil society. Key to this is for the state to recognise the need to engage society creatively on platforms that have organically evolved outside of it.
- Expansion of the economy and making growth inclusive: the growth path that fails to empower the majority mitigates against the developmental aspirations of a nation. We should admit that theoretical, ideological and political views on how best to expand the economy and ensure inclusive growth are varied and often divisive. The ability of the state to broker a lasting solution is critical.
- Building of key capabilities (human, physical and institutional): the state has to ensure that appropriately skilled personnel are recruited and retained in the right positions with authority and delegated responsibilities. Such personnel should be equipped with the right resources to manage state facilities and institutions without fear or favour. They should be insulated from undue political pressure. There should be a clear delineation of responsibilities between the key offices to

avoid unnecessary tensions dogging out departments, provinces, state owned enterprises, Chapter 9 institutions and municipalities. The state at various levels should be consistent in applying generally accepted principles, regulations and norms relating to the critical political, executive and administrative interfaces.

- Fostering strong leadership throughout society: a developmental state requires a development plan. A development plan requires a comprehensive implementation programme, but above all, the implementation programme requires political will and firm leadership. The state has to ensure that leadership is provided by all executing authorities, mayors, chairs of entities and all their accounting officers in a manner that is firm, fair and inclusive.

CLOSING

SIBUSISO VIL-NKOMO

Thank you very much. My job is quite easy and straightforward. Mine is to thank everybody but, before I do that, let me just make some very quick observations. I think the ANC was present in this room and people did not wave a flag and say 'I'm ANC'. What was done was that people spoke on how the ANC thought through the processes of change and also spoke about the fact that, in twenty years, this is what has been done and this is what is lacking. The other observation I made is that we had quite a number of presentations at this conference and all of these presentations led to very robust discussion. They led to serious interrogation of the issues of the day and matters of the future. Let us all celebrate the courage with which all of us had to confront the realities facing our fledgling democracy.

As South Africans, and also with the international community as well as our friends from other parts of the world, we have been able to create an environment where issues can be discussed openly and try to find solutions to the challenges. When I was growing up, we used to be told that Rome was not built in a day. One day I woke up and said apartheid will not die in a day, which means that we have a lot of work to do, the challenges are huge and the work to be done is ongoing into the foreseeable future. When Judge Moseneke spoke about 'What is to be Done?', quoting Vladimir Lenin, we also have to ask ourselves: 'How do We Create the Future?' Hence, the title of the conference is very apt. It actually gives us an opportunity to explore the future after twenty years of democracy.

I must also underscore something important. This venue was carefully selected. It was selected because the University of South Africa has a wonderful history. This institution graduated quite illustrious individuals, like Mr Ahmed Kathrada who was here yesterday – a contemporary of Nelson Mandela – Deputy President Cyril Ramaphosa, Justice Dikgang Moseneke, the late Mr Nelson Mandela, and many others.

So what the Mapungubwe Institute for Strategic Reflection (MISTRA) does, together with the Thabo Mbeki African Leadership Institute (TMALI), is to try and bring together great minds to a historic place to engage in useful thinking processes. Mr Vice Chancellor, I don't want to go through the list of your distinguished alumni but I want to pay particular attention to a group who I find to be very important for the present and the future: the young people who are today's students. You students have played a very important role in this conference. You asked the right questions. You were brave. I want to believe that out of this conference will emerge a number of serious research topics which you as students will have to pursue together with your mentors. It's important that you pay attention to that. This is a very special way in which MISTRA works: it works by using institutional memory and also incorporating new thinking from the young people. We believe that institutional memory and young or new knowledge or new thinking are very useful in creating a future for South Africa, the African continent and the world.

We have met our objectives. When the conference was being conceived there was thinking about having a conference which is forward looking. I think that has been achieved. More research has to be done in the context of that. We also debated understanding the historical moments which led to 1994. Historians must keep on writing about what was the momentum which drove the historical events that culminated as the 1994 settlement. You know, history, if you don't understand it, you will never understand the present and you will never understand the future.

It was important that that interrogation actually took place. I also think that a research agenda is emanating from this conference. It's a very important agenda. It is about the future; it is about South Africa's competitiveness in this part of the world and globally. So there must be very important research initiatives that are coming out of this conference.

I want to congratulate all the participants. Your presence was felt. We could see you engaging in all respects and we heard you pose the dynamic questions and recommendations. You have done well! We might have disagreed here and there but I think questions must be candidly put forward and the latter was certainly achieved. You must congratulate yourselves as the audience. Well done!

Let me also thank the Friedrich Ebert Foundation for having made the financial resources available to hold this outstanding conference. Without money these days it's difficult to orchestrate conferences of this kind. So we thank the Friedrich Ebert Foundation. They have always been there with us, even at the time of the multiparty negotiations and the bilaterals in the early 1990s. The FES funded quite a lot of the work which was being done to create the democratic South Africa we have and are celebrating today.

Members of the media, we thank you also. We have read some of the newspaper articles which have come out of the discussions of yesterday. We are happy about that, and you are stimulating debate by writing about the story of this conference. We had legal minds who played a critical role. Extremely bright minds and we thank all these outstanding individuals who were here.

You all know what the themes were, the reflections we were making, the critical reflections on the historic moments and the importance of reflections on the global economy. And also what's very important which I think came out of this, are reflections on what I consider to be the commanding height of the society which is the political economy. If we don't understand that, and if we don't interrogate and analyse this commanding height, I think the future will remain bleak.

Innovations and transdisciplinarity were well covered. Let me underscore that the future is bright for South Africa. However, this will not happen by itself. It is all dependent on the proper utilisation of our human capital and the production of useful development and scientific research. At MISTRA, we are convinced that reflection as well as excellent analyses are the cornerstones of relevant and usable research or experiential research. We underscore both the knowledge of discovery and the knowledge of invention. We also emphasise applied research. Just to deal with the two logics: *The logic of discovery* is what I am picking up when people talk about the developmental state. It seems to me there is an element of saying: we have discovered what we did not know exists. Developmental states have always existed and therefore there is nothing new about them but we have to interrogate that concept even further for it to be appropriate for South Africa's advancement. *Logic of invention* is when you come up with something new and I think MISTRA is also committed to the understanding of the logic of invention.

As I spoke about institutional memory, we must never underestimate its importance and existence in our society. We must capitalise on this wisdom in order to move South Africa ahead. The way forward for MISTRA and TMALI will be to produce a publication on what was discussed at this timely conference. We pride ourselves on making sure that what is discussed is also disseminated not only to South Africans but to the rest of the world for them to get to know that we do have thinkers; we do have people who conduct very good analysis in this part of the world.

The second important development or way forward which is coming out of the discussions of the last two days: MISTRA and TMALI will continue the discussions through roundtables and think-tanking sessions. We are not afraid to confront issues using these robust vehicles of communication and knowledge generation. One caution which I think is very important: we must avoid what scholars refer to as isomorphic mimicry, because if we engage in isomorphic mimicry then we create nothing new but we mimic what others have done well and done better and we will find ourselves not being able to be competitive with those who have done things better.

Finally, I want to congratulate the leadership and staff of TMALI, MISTRA and Unisa. You have all done a wonderful job of putting together this conference, and we believe that it's the beginning of things to come. This is not the end.

Thank you to everybody who is here. By the way, we had people from different parts of the world attending this important conference. We had people from different continents: our continent Africa, the Americas, Europe and Asia. So, well done! Let's keep on pushing.

CONTRIBUTORS

Deputy Chief Justice Dikgang Moseneke

Before his appointment as Justice of the Constitutional Court in November 2001, Moseneke was appointed a judge of the High Court in Pretoria. On 29 November 2002, he was appointed as judge in the Constitutional Court and in June 2005 he was appointed Deputy Chief Justice of the Republic of South Africa.

He is a founder member of the Black Lawyers' Association and of the National Association of Democratic Lawyers of South Africa.

In the past twenty years, Moseneke has read numerous papers at law and business conferences and published several academic papers in law journals at home and abroad.

Dr Frene Ginwala

Frene Noshir Ginwala was born in 1932 and studied law at the University of London in the United Kingdom (UK), where she completed her LLB degree. She returned to South Africa to complete her legal training, prior to the banning of the African National Congress (ANC). Ginwala worked in Tanzania, Zambia, Mozambique and the UK as an ANC official and as journalist and broadcaster in East Africa and Europe. She obtained a doctorate in history from Oxford University. Prior to her return from exile in 1990, Ginwala was head of the Political Research Unit in the Office of ANC President Oliver Tambo where she conducted research focusing on the transfer of military and nuclear technology.

She also served as ANC spokesperson in the UK on sanctions, the nuclear programme and the arms and oil embargoes relating to South Africa. Ginwala helped to set up the Women's National Coalition, which comprised organisations from across the political spectrum with the aim of drawing up a women's charter. She was elected national convener of the Coalition. She has held various influential positions in the ANC and other non-political organisations. Ginwala has been widely published on issues of democracy, good governance, human rights, human security, anti-apartheid and women's issues locally and abroad.

As Speaker of the National Assembly from 1994 until 2004, she was instrumental in arranging many significant changes in Parliament, including opening up a previously austere, racially exclusive, male-dominated and remote institution to the people at large. She commanded high respect amongst members of Parliament and the public in her tenure, which spanned the first critical decade of our democracy. Ginwala served as a member of the Preparatory Committee for the First World Conference of Presiding Officers. She was previously a board member of the International Institute for Democracy and Electoral Assistance as well as the former Chairperson of the Southern African Development Community Parliamentary Forum. She is a former member of the United Nations Secretary-General's Advisory Panel of High-Level Personalities on African Development and recently served as Commissioner of the International Commission on Human Security. Ginwala maintains her interest in promoting democracy, good governance, development and human rights, and human security.

Dr Sydney Mufamadi

Dr Sydney Mufamadi is the Director of the School of Leadership in the Faculty of Management at the University of Johannesburg. He is a lifelong opponent of apartheid who commenced his political activism in his teens.

He played a key role in the launch and maiden leadership of the Congress of South African Trade Unions (Cosatu) in 1985, represented the African National Congress (ANC) at the Convention for a Democratic South Africa (Codesa) in which the constitutional framework for the new South Africa was negotiated, and helped draft the National Peace Accord of 1991. In 1994, he was one of the two youngest members of cabinet at the age of thirty-five. He was appointed the foundation Minister for Safety and Security in the post-apartheid republic. Subsequently (1999–2008), he was twice appointed Minister for Provincial and Local Government.

He has been involved in mediation in Mozambique, Lesotho, the Democratic Republic of Congo and Zimbabwe. In addition, he has served as Expert Advisor to the African Union High-Level Panel on Darfur. His current research interests focus on the industrial policy and the political economy of war and peace in the Horn of Africa.

Professor Patricia McFadden

Professor Patricia McFadden is a member of the International Advisory Committee of the Thabo Mbeki African Leadership Institute and was an Extraordinary Visiting Professor of the Gender and Women's Studies Department at the University of the Western Cape in South Africa

(2011–2013). She is also a Life Associate and founding member at the Southern African Political Economy Series Trust.

Dr Miriam Altman

Dr Altman was appointed the Head of Strategy for the Telkom Group from 1 June 2013. She coordinates Telkom's strategic repositioning and turnaround, as well as Regulatory Affairs and Government Relations. She was previously Executive Director at the Human Sciences Research Council in South Africa. She is recognised as a leading economist, strategist and thought leader.

Miriam is a former Commissioner on the National Planning Commission in the Office of the Presidency. This body was established in 2010 to guide long-term planning for South Africa.

She has holds a BA in economics from McGill University, an M.Phil. from the University of Cambridge and a Ph.D. in economics from the University of Manchester. Dr Altman has produced more than 100 publications. She was commissioning editor of approximately 400 policy papers and publications in her division at the HSRC, and was guest editor of four special edition journals.

Dr Renosi Mokate

Dr Renosi Mokate was appointed Executive Director (ED) and Chief Executive Officer (CEO) of the Unisa Graduate School of Business Leadership (SBL) in January 2014. Before joining the SBL, Dr Mokate was an independent consultant for the Ministry of Finance and National Treasury as well as a member of the Investigation Steering Committee of the Municipal Demarcation Board.

From 2010 to 2012 she was the Executive Director of the World Bank Group (WB), where she represented Angola, Nigeria and South Africa and also served as the Chairperson of the Audit Committee as well as member of various other committees. Prior to that she was Deputy Governor (DG) of the South African Reserve Bank (SARB). During her tenure as DG she was a member of the Monetary Policy Committee, the Governors' Executive Committee and the Audit Committee.

She also chaired two subsidiaries of the SARB, namely the South African Bank Note Company (Pty) Ltd and the SA Mint (Pty) Ltd. She has held various positions in the public sector and academia, including being the Chairperson and CEO of the Financial and Fiscal Commission; CEO of the

Central Energy Fund; ED: Group Economic and Social Analysis, Human Sciences Research Council (HSRC); Director and Professor: Centre for Reconstruction and Development, University of Pretoria; Senior Policy Analyst, Development Bank of Southern Africa; and Associate Professor of Economics at Lincoln University, Pennsylvania, USA.

She is a member of the Board of Advisors, School of Public Policy and Administration, University of Delaware, USA and the Advisory Panel on the Development Progress Report, Overseas Development Institute, United Kingdom.

She has held numerous board positions in the public and private sectors. She is also a board member of the Bidvest Bank as well as Vukile Property Fund. More recently, Renosi Mokate was appointed the Chairperson of South Africa's Government Employees Pension Fund.

She holds a Ph.D. and MA from the University of Delaware, Newark, Delaware and a BA from Lincoln University, Pennsylvania. Her areas of specialisation are Development Economics, Urban Economics and Policy Analysis. She has received various awards including the Founders Day Award from Lincoln University as well as the Presidential Citation from the University of Delaware.

Professor Vusi Gumede

Vusi Gumede is Professor and Head of the Thabo Mbeki African Leadership Institute at the University of South Africa. He previously was an associate professor at the University of Johannesburg. He also lectures public policy, since 2009, at the Graduate School of Public and Development Management of the University of Witwatersrand (now called the Wits School of Governance) in South Africa. He also facilitates, since 2010, the National School of Governance modules in economics and policy analysis, through the Vaal University of Technology and through the Wits School of Governance.

Over and above being Chairman of Southern Africa Trust, he is also a Fellow of the Mapungubwe Institute for Strategic Reflection, Fellow at the Institute of Justice & Reconciliation, Commissioner for the City of Tshwane Planning Commission and editor for the *Journal of African Studies and Development*.

He worked for the South African government, in various capacities, for about 12 years – he was Chief Policy Analyst, among other things, in The Presidency. He has been hosted by the Institute for African Development at

Cornell University as Distinguished Africanist Scholar and by Yale University as Yale World Fellow. He has spent research fellowships with universities in Europe and the United States, and more recently with the University of Botswana.

He holds postgraduate qualifications in economics and policy studies, including a Ph.D. in economics (2003). He publishes in areas of macroeconomics and political economy in various journals and through book chapters in co-edited books.

Trevor Manuel

Trevor Manuel served as a cabinet minister from 1994 to 2014 under the first four presidents of democratic South Africa: Mandela, Mbeki, Motlanthe and Zuma. He was first appointed to Cabinet as Minister of Trade and Industry in May 1994, a portfolio he held for two years. In April 1996, he became Finance Minister, steering the South African economy for thirteen years as one of the world's longest-serving finance ministers. During his last term in office, he served as Minister in the Presidency responsible for the National Planning Commission, a position he held from May 2009 to May 2014. As Chairperson of the Commission, he oversaw the drafting of the broadly accepted and first National Development Plan for the country. He served on the National Executive Committee of the African National Congress from July 1991 to December 2012, and on its National Working Committee from 1991 to 1994.

During his Ministerial career, Mr Manuel assumed a number of ex officio positions in international bodies, including the United Nations Conference on Trade and Development (UNCTAD), the World Bank, the International Monetary Fund (IMF), the G20, the African Development Bank, and the Southern African Development Community (SADC). He was elected by his peers as Chair of a number of these bodies and also served two terms as Chairperson of the Development Committee of the World Bank.

Mr Manuel has received a number of awards and presentations, including Africa's Finance Minister of the Year and the Woodrow Wilson Public Service award. He has seven honorary doctorates from South African tertiary institutions and a Doctor of Laws from MacMaster University, Ontario, Canada. He has served as the Chancellor of the Cape Peninsula University of Technology (CPUT) since May 2008. In September 2014, he announced that he would be joining the Rothschild Group as a senior advisor to the Group worldwide and Deputy Chairman of Rothschild in South Africa.

Judge Albie Sachs

On turning six, during World War II, Albie Sachs received a card from his father expressing the wish that he would grow up to be a soldier in the fight for liberation.

His career in human rights activism started at the age of seventeen when, as a second year law student at the University of Cape Town, he took part in the Defiance of Unjust Laws Campaign. Three years later he attended the Congress of the People at Kliptown where the Freedom Charter was adopted. He started practice as an advocate at the Cape Bar aged twenty-one. The bulk of his work involved defending people charged under racist statutes and repressive security laws. Many faced the death sentence. He himself was raided by the security police, subjected to banning orders restricting his movement and eventually placed in solitary confinement without trial for two prolonged spells of detention.

In 1966, he went into exile. After spending eleven years studying and teaching law in England, he worked for a further eleven years in Mozambique as law professor and legal researcher. In 1988 he was blown up by a bomb placed in his car in Maputo by South African security agents, losing an arm and the sight of an eye.

During the 1980s, working closely with Oliver Tambo, leader of the ANC in exile, he helped draft the organisation's Code of Conduct, as well as its statutes. After recovering from the bomb he devoted himself full-time to preparations for a new democratic constitution for South Africa. In 1990, he returned home and, as a member of the Constitutional Committee and the National Executive of the ANC, took an active part in the negotiations which led to South Africa becoming a constitutional democracy. After the first democratic election in 1994, he was appointed by President Nelson Mandela to serve on the newly established Constitutional Court.

In addition to his work on the Court, he has travelled to many countries sharing South African experience in healing divided societies. He has also been engaged in the sphere of art and architecture, and played an active role in the development of the Constitutional Court building and its art collection on the site of the Old Fort Prison in Johannesburg.

Pregs Govender

Pregaluxmi Govender is Deputy Chairperson of South Africa's Human Rights Commission. An activist against apartheid since 1974, she taught

English in Durban, at schools and at university, before joining the trade union movement in the 1980s. She was National Educator of the Garment and Allied Workers' Union (GAWU) (now The Southern African Clothing and Textile Workers' Union [SACTWU]) before heading South Africa's first Workers' College. Pregs served on the executive structures of Cosatu's National Gender Committee and the UDF-affiliated Natal Organisation of Women.

During the negotiated transition, Pregs managed the Women's National Coalition, which mobilised rural and urban women to impact on South Africa's Constitution. She then worked in the national Reconstruction and Development (RDP) office, integrating women's concerns into the RDP. As an ANC member, she was elected to the National Assembly in South Africa's first democratic election. In the '94 budget debates she initiated SA's gender budgeting and steered its impact on the '98/'99 National Budget. In '94 she was tasked with editing SA's Country Report to Beijing.

Pregs was elected Chairperson of Parliament's Committee on Women where she served from 1996 to 2002. This Committee ensured that 80 per cent of its legislative priorities were enacted by 1999. After being the only MP to register opposition to the arms deal in the Defence Budget Vote, Pregs resigned from Parliament in 2002. Her work thereafter included being the Chairperson of the Independent Panel Review of Parliament. Her human rights activism includes being a member of the global Panel on Human Dignity. Pregs' awards include honorary doctorates in Law and Philosophy, the first Ruth First Fellowship and the Fulbright New Century Scholarship for the Global Empowerment of Women.

She has authored many papers and articles and contributed to several publications. Pregs is the author of *Love and Courage, a Story of Insubordination.*

Mazibuko Jara

Mr Jara currently works as a Senior Researcher at the UCT Law, Race and Gender Research Unit – Traditional Courts Bill. He is also an Associate Editor of *Amandla!*, a bi-monthly magazine that was launched in 2007. He holds an M.Phil. degree from the University of the Western Cape (UWC), and is presently conducting doctoral research on the political economy of the food regime in South Africa through UWC.

Previously, he was employed as a Project Coordinator and then National Director at the National Coalition for Gay and Lesbian Equality.

Professor Tshilidzi Marwala

Professor Tshilidzi Marwala is Deputy Vice-Chancellor of Research at the University of Johannesburg and an Independent Non-Executive Director for EOH Holdings. He is a Member of the South African Academy of Engineering, the World Academy of Science and South African Academy of South Africa. He has published eight books on artificial intelligence, supervised forty-three Masters and eighteen Ph.D. students to completion.

Dr Hester du Plessis

Before joining MISTRA as Faculty Head Humanity, Dr du Plessis held research positions at various research institutions including as associate researcher at the Sustainable Energy Technology and Research (SeTAR) Centre, University of Johannesburg, and senior research specialist at the Human Sciences Research Council (HSRC) in Pretoria.

Erika Kraemer-Mbula

Erika Kraemer-Mbula is a Senior Lecturer and Research Fellow at the Institute for Economic Research at Tshwane University of Technology (South Africa), co-hosting the DST-NRF Centre of Excellence in Scientometrics and STI Policy. Erika's research interests are on innovation systems and the expansion of creative competencies through technological learning, public policy and international cooperation in Science, Technology and Innovation, and their implications for sustainable and equitable development in Africa.

Professor Mammo Muchie

Professor Mammo Muchie, originally from Ethiopia, obtained his D.Phil. in Science and Technology from the University of Sussex, United Kingdom, in 1986. He started his career at the University of Columbia as lecturer in physics and mathematics. Later, he joined a number of other institutions such as the Ethiopian Standards Institute, Sussex University, Middlesex University, University of Amsterdam, University of Maastricht and many more, sharing his knowledge of and expertise in economic sciences, humanities and social sciences.

Currently, Professor Muchie is the holder of the SARCHi Research Chair and Research Director of DIIPER on Innovation in Aalborg University, Aalborg Graduate School of International Studies, Centre for Comparative Integration as well as chairman of the Network of Ethiopian Scholars and a regular international visiting professor.

Imraan Patel

Imraan Patel is a public policy and strategy manager with a focus on innovation, inclusive development, sustainability, social and economic development, public management and governance.

Employed since 2006 at the South African Department of Science and Technology, he currently holds the position of Deputy Director-General: Socio-Economic Partnerships and represents the department on the social and economic clusters of government and the advisory committee for the Green Fund. He is also a member of the board of MINTEK, the Water Research Commission, and the Southern African Science Service Centre for Climate Change and Adaptive Land Management (SASSCAL).

Just prior to joining the DST, he worked for four years at the Centre for Public Service Innovation, an agency of government supporting innovation in the delivery of public services. He also worked at the Department of Public Service and Administration for four years. He began his working life with a five-year stint at the Workplace Information Group (WIG), a non-governmental organisation providing health and safety support to trade unions followed by a three-year employment in the formative years of the National Labour and Economic Development Institute (NALEDI), a think tank to Cosatu, the largest trade union federation in South Africa.

At the DST, he is responsible for strategically driving a portfolio of investments and policies that advance the social and economic development priorities of government through science and technology-based interventions. Areas of focus include Information and Communications Technologies, Sector Development, Climate Change and Biodiversity, Environmental Goods and Services with a focus on water and waste, Advanced Manufacturing, Mining and Minerals Beneficiation, Chemicals, Technology Localisation, Innovation for Inclusive Development, and indicators and measurement of systems of innovation.

Parks Tau

Parks Tau is Mayor for the City of Johannesburg. He was elected President of the Soweto Youth Congress and later served on the Pretoria Witwatersrand Vereeniging (PWV) region of the newly launched ANC Youth League in 1990. He served as Regional Secretary of the ANC Johannesburg region and is currently the Regional Deputy Chairperson.

Raenette Taljaard

Ms Taljaard is a part-time commissioner of the Electoral Commission of South Africa and senior lecturer, Public Policy, University of Cape Town.

She holds a BA (Hons) in Law; MA in International Relations, University of Johannesburg, and MSc in Public Policy and Public Administration, London School of Economics. From 1999–2004, she was Member of South African Parliament, including, from 2002 to 2004, as Shadow Minister of Finance.

Ms Taljaard is a Yale World Fellow; Fellow Emerging Leaders Program, Duke University and UCT; and African Leadership Initiative Fellow, Aspen Institute. She lectures and writes on private military and private security companies and political accountability questions.

Ms Taljaard served as Director of the Helen Suzman Foundation from 2006 to 2009 and she is a Young Global Leader of the World Economic Forum and serves on the World Economic Forum Global Agenda Council for Africa.

Pascal Moloi

Pascal Moloi is a former member of the National Planning Commission. He is the Director of Modiro Consulting. He has held an extensive number of senior leadership positions in the public sector. His areas of expertise are Public Sector Management, Change Management and Organisational/ Institutional Design.

Professor Sibusiso Vil-Nkomo

Sibusiso Vil-Nkomo is Chairperson of the Board of Governors of the Mapungubwe Institute for Strategic Reflection (MISTRA) and Senior Research Professor at the Centre for the Advancement of Scholarship at the University of Pretoria. From 2011 to 2012 he was a J. William Fulbright Research Scholar in the Department of Economics at Fordham University as well as a Fellow of the Fordham School of Business Consortium in New York City. He is a former member of the Executive of the University of Pretoria and Dean of the Faculty of Economic and Management Sciences. He was a Public Service Commissioner under President Nelson Mandela.

Professor Vil-Nkomo was Associate Professor at Lincoln University in Pennsylvania and co-taught with Professors Ann Seidman and Robert Seidman at Clark University in Massachusetts. He was Visiting Professor at the Andrew Young School of Policy Studies at Georgia State University and he is a member of the Academy of Science in South Africa and the South African Association of Public Administration and Management. Professor Vil-Nkomo's research interests are in urban economics, public sector economics, human capital investment and the political economy of development. He has published extensively.